Angel Inspiration

Angel Inspiration

HOW TO CHANGE YOUR WORLD WITH THE ANGELS

DIANA COOPER

Hodder & Stoughton

I would like to dedicate this book to my wonderful daughter, Lauren,
with thanks for all her support and for choosing me as a mother.

First published in Great Britain in 2001 by Hodder and Stoughton
A division of Hodder Headline
This paperback edition published in 2004

A Mobius paperback

9

A CIP catalogue record for this title is available from
the British Library.

ISBN 978 0 340 83509 8

Typeset in Sabon by Palimpsest Book Production Limited,
Polmont, Stirlingshire
Printed and bound in the UK by
CPI Mackays, Chatham ME5 8TD

Hodder Headline's policy is to use papers that are natural, renewable
and recyclable products and made from wood grown in sustainable
forests. The logging and manufacturing processes are expected to
conform to the environmental regulations of the country of origin

Hodder and Stoughton Ltd
A division of Hodder Headline
338 Euston Road
London NW1 3BH

Contents

Angel Meditations and Exercises

Introduction

At the age of forty-two, I was getting divorced and was at the bottom of a deep black emotional pit. Despite having no religious or spiritual background, I called out for help from the depth of my soul and my Guardian Angel appeared to me and showed me my future. This changed my life.

My angel's love and strength enabled me to release the past and start a new life. I trained as a hypno-therapist and healer and devoted my life to my spiritual path. For years I saw individual clients but, although I was aware of angelic presences, I connected mainly with my spirit guides.

Eleven years later, the angel returned and asked me to undertake a mission. I was to introduce angels to people. I was reluctant to do this but eventually agreed. Once again my life changed. From that time angels surrounded me and helped me in my quest to draw attention to their presence.

Without my telling anyone what had happened, the size of my classes immediately doubled. People started flocking to my workshops in increasing numbers, sent by their angels.

They impressed on me to write my next book about angels. I did so with joy and it was completed very quickly. The angels told me which publisher to send it

to, which day to post it, and that it was to be published for Christmas. Against all the odds, it was.

Source is sending His angels, who are His messengers, to Earth in greater numbers than ever before. The first surge was sent in biblical times. A second surge was directed here in medieval days, and now we are blessed to be here during the third mass appearance of angels on Earth.

The Dean of an English cathedral told me that he was taught at theological college that angels were a figment of the medieval imagination. When he read my book, he said to himself, 'No! Surely angels can't do those things.' So he said aloud, 'If there are angels, will you turn all the traffic lights green on my journey today?' He was travelling some fifty miles. When he returned, he phoned me and told me in amazement, 'They did.' Throughout his journey the traffic lights turned green as he approached them. I have to add that I met him for lunch on a couple of occasions and he was a very special person.

We humans are only now opening up to the presence of angels. They promise us that there will be mass sightings within the next twenty years. We are privileged to be on Earth during this incredible opportunity for spiritual growth.

Angels are very high-frequency beings, divine messengers, guides and healers who have no free will of their own. They only carry out the will of God.

Everyone has their own Guardian Angel, who is with them throughout all their incarnations. Angels are waiting and longing to help you, but under Spiritual

Law they cannot do so unless you ask them to. The moment you ask, they are delighted to assist you, protect you and smooth your path whenever possible. They also wait to carry out your commands, which enable them to heal the world.

Your Guardian Angel is with you at all times, lovingly radiating light towards you. Other angels are near you. So are your helpers, who are usually loved ones and ancestors who have died. Your spirit guides are with you. As you evolve, greater guides, Ascended Masters and even Archangels surround you. Your invisible companions are constantly drawing you towards your destiny. They create a powerful current and when you relax into this divine guidance, your life flows. They sweep you through challenges and round problems. It is when you resist and want do it your way that you have pains in your body and get stuck in your difficulties.

Because humans have free will, angels cannot do their work without your cooperation. Humans are the intermediaries through which angels channel their energy on Earth. As you offer to work with them, they come close to you, waiting for you to direct them.

As soon as you ask the angels to assist a person or situation, your thoughts and words create the bridges which allow them to reach in and help. Without your intercession they could not do so.

When several people together invoke the angels to touch and raise a situation, the angelic force is enormous and miracles become possible. Together, humans and angels have the power to change the world.

When the angels asked me to work with them and to introduce them to people, I started to invoke their help and assistance for myself and others. The change in my life was instant as abundance of every kind flowed to me.

Soon after their appearance I attended a workshop in another town. Several of the participants were staying in the same bed and breakfast as I was and, unbeknown to me, our landlady was a medium, who saw spirit. After breakfast on Sunday morning she pointed to me accusingly and said, 'You, the lady in blue, you brought a lot of angels with you and they have been waiting around in my house and garden all weekend!' This was probably the first time I realized that *when you dedicate your life to service, angels approach you in the hope that you will direct them with your thoughts, to help and heal all on Earth*.

Now I am sometimes accompanied by thousands of angels, especially when I am facilitating a workshop, for we always send the angels to help the world. Many people have written to me and told me that as soon as they started to direct angels to heal the planet, an infinite number flocked to work with them.

When you dedicate your life to a spiritual path, the angels will find ways of helping your mission. After I wrote *A Little Light on Angels*, I was invited to appear on a well-known TV programme. Just before I went on air, the presenters and I were asked if we would have our auras photographed. Naturally I agreed. Automatically I asked my angels to step into the picture for the photograph, thinking that their light would be able to touch people through the photo.

Little did I imagine that the angels would impress themselves on to the aura photo, so that the viewers would be able to see their image clearly behind me. How incredible the angels are! As a result of this, the programme was deluged with calls and I was asked to return the following day. That aura photo, with my angels standing behind me, has appeared on television programmes throughout the world and each time there is an unprecedented response. Angels can help your life and your purpose in ways that you would not even conceive possible!

If the angels think that something is important, they will wake me in the middle of the night and impress on me what to do.

On one occasion I was staying in California and had a lunch appointment the following day with Dawn Fazende, the editor of the *Mount Shasta Magazine*. At 4.45 a.m. I was woken by the angels who informed me that the meeting was very important and told me exactly what I must say to her. The moment Dawn and I met we knew it was to be a special connection. We joined hands to bless our meal and were both held in a force-field of love and light, so powerful that we could not move. I have never experienced the like.

Dawn wrote an article containing all the information the angels wanted to impart. Furthermore I now contribute a regular angel column to her beautiful magazine. In this way the angels are becoming even better known in America. They have incredible ways of making sure the Will of God is done!

*

I had nearly finished writing a spiritual novel when my publisher asked me to write another angel book. I said I would think about it but had little intention of doing so. At three o'clock the following morning I was woken from a deep sleep, with angels all round me. I was filled with a wonderful sense of joy and delight at the thought of writing this book.

They told me to remind you how much they can help you. In turn you can use your divine power to direct them to heal the world.

I knew I must start immediately and they have helped me all the way. Here it is.

Angels

CHAPTER ONE

Guardian Angels

You have a Guardian Angel who is appointed to you when you first incarnate and stays with you throughout all your incarnations, evolving as you evolve. Like all angels it is androgynous and is pure spirit.

Your Guardian Angel holds the vision of your divine perfection and reminds you of this constantly. He whispers to you of harmony, truth and integrity. If you are in dispute with someone, your Guardian Angel is holding hands with the other person's angel, in perfect love. If you cannot resolve a problem, he holds the vision of the highest outcome, making it possible for you to achieve it. However badly you behave, he loves you unconditionally.

Your Guardian Angel wants to help you but under Spiritual Law cannot do so unless you ask. His greatest delight is to smooth your life. Nothing is too small or too large. For example, he will help you to shop for perfect presents, drive safely, or introduce you to someone who can help you. Your Guardian Angel brings about synchronicities and meetings in your life.

If it is not your destiny to suffer or your time to die, your Guardian Angel will step in and save you.

Mary Davies always connects with her Guardian Angel, who looks after her. Her tooth broke when she and her

3

husband were on holiday. It was after six o'clock in the evening. Everything was shut and her tooth was beginning to hurt badly. She did not know where she could get help, so she sat in the car and asked her Guardian Angel.

Mary and her husband drove into the next village, where they found a small hospital and stopped to ask if there was a local dentist. The receptionist phoned round for Mary and found that there was a dentist round the corner. Someone had not turned up for her appointment and he could see her immediately.

Mary added with a smile that she had still got the temporary filling he put in for her.

On another occasion Mary and her husband were returning home by train. As always she asked the angels to protect her journey. When the train was travelling at full speed, the window behind them shattered. It was assumed that a brick had been thrown from a bridge. They were covered in glass but incredibly neither of them was hurt in any way.

She said thank you to her Guardian Angel for saving them from injury.

My friend Denis has been saved from death several times by his Guardian Angel. On one occasion when he was riding his bicycle, he turned right in front of a car which he had not seen. He felt held by a presence and missed death by a hair's-breadth.

The second incident also occurred when he was riding his bike. This time it was a rainy day on a slippery road and he was thrown off his bicycle and into the path of a huge oncoming lorry. He lay in the road helplessly watching the wheels getting closer and closer to his head. Within an inch of him, the lorry stopped.

When asked why he stopped the driver said that he had no idea that anyone was under his lorry but he had an irresistible 'impulse' to stop. He felt he was not alone in the cab although in physical terms he was.

On each of these occasions Denis was able to ride off quite calmly as though nothing untoward had happened.

On another occasion he fell asleep at the wheel and woke to find a golden being driving the car. She disappeared when he opened his eyes.

I think we can safely say that his Guardian Angel is making sure he stays around to complete his mission on Earth!

Your Guardian Angel is literally the keeper of your conscience and will prompt you to do what is right. He will pop thoughts into your mind. If you are angry with someone and intend to have it out with them, he will try to help you see things from a higher perspective.

Sherren Mayes told me that while she was on holiday, she lent her flat to a girl who came to her healing and psychic development class. When she discovered that this girl wore her clothes, had friends to stay and left her flat in a mess, she was enraged. She was all set to have it out with her but a clear voice said to Sherren, 'Be kind to her. Don't be angry. Look for the higher perspective and see the good in her.' Sherren was so stunned that she said nothing to the girl. In fact she was very kind to her.

Later Sherren realized that if she had shouted at her, the girl would have stopped coming to the class. Then

she would not have developed her psychic and healing ability. She also introduced many people to Sherren and her classes, which enabled them to be helped on their way.

Many sensitive people find it hard to stay grounded and fully present in life. I was intrigued when two people within a week told me that their Guardian Angel had helped them find a way to ground.

One was 'flipping out' and when she called out for help she saw angels pouring glue round her feet, which helped considerably.

The other, Debbie Mann, constantly felt so ungrounded that, before she went to bed, she told her Guardian Angel that she seemed to be blind and deaf to his guidance, and would he please stick something in front of her nose so that she could learn the lesson! She wrote, 'Next morning when I woke up I automatically did something I never do. I picked up *A Little Light on the Spiritual Laws* to read it, though usually I only read in the evening. I opened it at 'The Law of Resistance'. Since then I have been doing an affirmation dance, with arms high and welcoming and stamping my feet. I sing, "I am healthy and grounded." It works. The angels have showered me with angel light and I feel GREAT.'

If your Guardian Angel cannot help you directly, he will produce a book with an answer in it, or impress on you to turn on the radio or TV in time to hear what you need to know. Always follow those impulses and impressions. They come from your Guardian Angel.

It really does not matter whether you pray directly to

God for help or talk to your angel. Your angel is the intermediary between you and Source, who deals with your requests anyway. However, it is really wonderful to have a personal relationship with your angel and it helps to know his name. A name has a vibration, and calling your angel by his name enables you to feel closer. His name can be anything from a down-to-earth Fred to an exotic-sounding Auroriol or the name of an Archangel, like Gabriel.

Your aura is the electromagnetic field, which surrounds you and is influenced by your thoughts. If you are sending out rage and hate your aura will most likely be full of red and black daggers.

It is very difficult for angels to connect with you if your emotions are upset and discordant. They can help you more easily if your aura is calm and golden, so if you wish to connect with your Guardian Angel, take time to centre yourself and breathe the colour gold around you before you talk to him.

Service work
Sit quietly and direct your Guardian Angel to help other people. Then ask for help for yourself.

CHAPTER TWO

Angelic Assistance

Angels come to us in three circumstances. The first is when you send out a cry from the depth of your soul. They can then help you on the ray of compassion under the Law of Grace. This is what happened to me when I cried out for help when I was at the bottom of an emotional pit. My angel appeared and showed me my destiny. I then had to work tirelessly to achieve it.

When the soul is calling, the person is ready to change his or her life. The angels can then intervene. However, if you cry out from neediness and frustration, your plea comes from ego. Were the angels to rescue your ego, you would not change your ways. Therefore they cannot help.

Second, if it is not your time to die or be injured, your angel will step in and save you. If you are about to undergo a traumatic experience, which your soul does not need, he will intervene.

Angels cannot interfere with the blueprint of your life, so if your contract is to die as a child or young adult, they must let it happen. Your angel must also bow to the dictates of your higher self. This means that if your soul wants you to have a wake-up call such as an illness, accident or financial disaster, your angel has to stand by with love and compassion and allow you to experience it.

At one seminar a woman shared with us her experience in a car which skidded on black ice on the motorway. The car veered off out of control into the cones by the central barrier. She watched in awe as an angel took the steering wheel. The car did a 360-degree turn and was back safely in position on the road. The angel then vanished.

Angels frequently save you from danger but only very rarely do you see them and become aware of their presence.

A farmer told me of a time when he had a lot of business problems. Everything seemed to be going wrong and he was in despair. One windy night the cows got out. He traipsed out in the dark and searched for hours but still he could not get them all back. At last, exhausted, he sat down in the shed, with his head in his hands. He was ready to fall asleep.

Suddenly something hit from behind and a voice said, 'Things will be alright.' He knew it was his Guardian Angel and from that moment everything went right.

Third, your angel can help you if you ask. He cannot save you from the outcome of your stupidity or greed or hastiness, so if, for instance, you decide to marry someone totally inappropriate or to put your money into a ridiculous business venture, you must bear the consequences. No higher being would take away your karma for it is your opportunity for growth. But when you have grown through the experience or learnt the lesson, you can ask your angel to mitigate the effects of your decisions and actions. He will help you to bring new and better things into your life.

The angelic beings will also assist you on a day-to-day basis to smooth your life, if you ask for help. Get into the habit of asking for small things as well as big ones and you will be amazed at the results.

The way in which you ask is important. I have hundreds of letters from people who tell me that they are desperately asking their angels all the time. Sometimes they are screaming for help or sobbing and miserable. This is akin to a needy child constantly demanding an ice-cream. It is asking an angel to satisfy your ego.

So if you wish to ask your angel to help, let your request come from a calm, centred, wise space within you. Ask, expecting there to be a response. Trust that help is there and it will be.

Guardian Angels bring people together and synchronize their needs.

Greg was in his office, feeling totally overloaded. They urgently needed another computer programmer to fill a vacancy and had not even had time to advertise. Suddenly he remembered the angels. He shut his door, closed his eyes and quietly and clearly told the angels what help he needed. A few minutes later his phone rang and he almost did not answer it as he was so busy. However, it rang persistently and when he finally picked up the receiver, it was the perfect person for the job, who had heard in a very obscure way about the vacancy. This man had all the qualifications and experience needed. Most important of all, he could start immediately.

A lady told me that her fountain in the garden pond stopped and she thought the fish would die. She couldn't fix it. Several people tried to mend it but nothing worked. She went to bed, expecting that all the fish would be dead in the morning. However, before she went to sleep she asked the angels to help with the fountain. She woke to the sound of running water. The fish were fine and the fountain has worked ever since.

If, under Spiritual Law, the angels can help, they will. If not, you must deal with the problem in a physical way. That is then your challenge, something you must learn. Do get into the habit of asking the angels first, before you call the plumber, the mechanic or a friend. It costs nothing, saves hours of frustration and builds your faith.

Call out for help for yourself or others the moment you sense danger. The angels will respond in whatever way they can. Here is a story I was told on a workshop.

Bronwen was on holiday and was relaxing in the hotel gardens. Her daughter was in the swimming pool. Suddenly she felt a thump in her solar plexus and knew something was wrong with her child. *Immediately she called out to the angels to help her daughter* and ran to the swimming pool.

Her daughter had been in the middle of the pool. She had swallowed water and was choking and sinking. Suddenly she felt herself being lifted by unseen hands to the ladder at the side. Then her mother arrived on the scene and was able to lift her out safely.

Even though you can see or sense nothing, the angels look after you when you ask them to.

Carlyn Rafferty read *A Little Light on Angels* and decided to ask the angels to look after her, her husband and her son Lewis, who was two.

A few days later, Lewis tripped and went head-first through a glass door. Carlyn picked the glass out of his head. He did not have one cut or drop of blood, although the pane of glass was totally smashed. She wrote, 'If that is not the work of his Guardian Angel then I don't know whatever will be.'

John told me that he woke in the middle of the night to find that his brother was not at home. He just knew something was wrong. We all have a gut instinct about these things. So he sent the angels to help his brother.

When he went downstairs in the morning he found that his brother's motorbike was outside the house, completely mangled. Later his brother told him that he had crashed into a car, but he had been picked up and landed very softly. He had been completely unhurt.

When you ask for help for someone the thoughts you send out create a bridge of light which the angels can use to help that person.

I laughed when a friend told me that his office cleaner said to him, 'Of course there are Guardian Angels. None of my boys would have survived without them.'

Service work
Sit quietly and direct angels to help individuals in need.

CHAPTER THREE

Talking to Someone Else's Angel

Your Guardian Angel holds your divine blueprint. This means that he carries the imprint of the highest potential for your life. At all times he stands beside you, radiating towards you the possibility of dealing with everything in a perfect way.

He can help you in a million ways but you have to ask for that help. Under Spiritual Law no Being of Light can change things unless you ask. You must listen. Angelic love and guidance are available to you at all times.

Your Guardian Angel is standing by without judgement, watching you take less than helpful decisions, quarrelling with someone or making a mess of an aspect of your life. He can only whisper higher guidance to you in the trust that one day you will pause and hear it.

The Guardian Angels of everyone connected to you are also holding the blueprint of their divine perfection up to them. When your angels work together, it is surprising what happens. If you are in conflict with someone, it is helpful to sit quietly and ask your angel to talk to the other person's angel. It really does not matter how big or small the problem is.

Naturally no angel will communicate your anger, hurt, fears or negative energies of any description. Nor are desperate, emotionally charged pleas helpful. Make sure you are calm and centred before you ask, make your request from the highest motive and know that all the angels concerned are doing all that is possible. They cannot force someone to hear.

We did the following exercise at a talk I gave. I asked everyone to close their eyes and think of someone with whom they would like a better relationship. Then I invited them to tell their angel that they would like to resolve this problem and enjoy a harmonious relationship with the person concerned. The next step was to ask their angel to communicate a message of reconciliation and love to the other person's angel.

A few days later one man told me that he had a great deal of difficulty relating to a particular lady who also attended the talk. She ignored him or was abrupt with him to the point of rudeness. So he asked his angel to talk to hers to help resolve the difficulty. At the end of the evening she came up to him, put her arm on his and was totally charming to him.

A few days later he was at a meeting. A colleague, who would never meet his eye or speak to him unless he had to, was there. So he quietly asked his angel to communicate a message of peace and friendship to this man. In the tea-break the man smiled at him and called out, 'Can I get you a cup of tea?'

Asking your angel to communicate with someone else's angel can soothe the mosquito bites in relationships. It can also help to heal the wasp stings.

On one workshop we asked our Guardian Angel to communicate with someone else's angel about something really important to us.

A few weeks later I had a letter from a lady whose three adult stepchildren refused to accept her. They would not come to the home she shared with their father and were rude and abusive whenever they met. It caused her grief and tension and disrupted the extended family.

She was at her wits' end when she attended the workshop. She told her Guardian Angel about the problem and directed him to speak to the angels of her three stepchildren, sending them a message of loving acceptance and telling them it was safe to let down their attack. She did not want to take their mother's place or hurt them. She asked their angels to hold out the hand of friendship to them.

None of them had been in contact for some time. So she was amazed and delighted when both her stepdaughters phoned the following day. Both of them were more than relaxed and civil to her. She said they had a lovely conversation. Her stepson e-mailed a few days later and proposed a visit. She continued to communicate via his Guardian Angel and the visit was an outstanding success.

Angels really can open doors which seem closed.

Another lady used angel-to-angel communication with even more startling results. For seven years she had a double load at work. There had been an ongoing battle with her boss about this and nothing changed.

So she talked to her angel about it and directed him to take a message to her boss's Guardian Angel saying that she really did need some help. She made this communication on a Sunday. She wrote, 'Within an hour of my arrival at work on Monday, my boss arrived to

inform me that I needed an assistant. Who did I want, etc.? He couldn't come earlier because he had been at a meeting.'

He confided to her that the idea had come to him the previous evening! Within a week of calling on her angel to talk to his, she had a bigger office and an assistant.

It only takes a moment to ask your angel to communicate with someone else's. The results can be incredible.

It does not have to be someone you know. You can tell your angel to talk to the President or Prime Minister's angel, or to the Guardian Angel of a despot or the big boss of a company, and ask their angel to help them make decisions for the highest good or to take humanitarian actions.

When you communicate through divine forces, you become a powerful light.

Service work
Sit quietly and direct your angel to talk to the angel of someone who is influential in the world about taking decisions for the highest good of all.

You can tell the angel to remind them about environmental issues, health, empowerment of others, integrity or any higher way of being.

CHAPTER FOUR

Angel Signals

Angels use synchronicity and coincidence to give you signals about your life path and their presence. They also work in mysterious and magical ways to push projects forward. Here is an incredible story of a recurring dream which guided a friend of mine towards his mission.

My friend Ken Peacock was suffering from a frozen shoulder. He went to a spiritual healer who was working on his body when she was amazed to see that an angel was stopping the healing energy from reaching his shoulder. She had never seen an angel before.

She told him that he must seek another way of healing his shoulder. So he went to his doctor who confirmed the frozen shoulder and referred him for physiotherapy at the local hospital.

He had never been to this hospital before and after his appointment he stopped to look at the outside of the building. It was built on one level. The wards were separated from each other so that it looked like a train with eleven carriages. The incredible building was completely unique. *And Ken recognized it immediately. The building had appeared to him in a vivid, recurring dream for the past thirty years*. In the dream he felt he owned the building and it was clearer in his mind's eye than his own home. He had been searching for it for years.

Now, thanks to the angel, he had found it. However,

he discovered to his dismay that only the physiotherapy department remained open. Everything else had been closed down and centralized. The magnificent hospital, surrounded by gracious trees, was about to be demolished and the land sold for housing. It was owned by the National Health Service, which had spent several million pounds building two state-of-the-art operating theatres which had never been used.

From that moment Ken decided to set about saving the hospital of his dream. He prepared a business proposal to use the beautiful building as a profitable and successful integrated hospital. When it was ready he phoned the Chairman of the Trustees for the hospital company, who told him that the National Health Service had rejected their plans without consultation.

Ken told him of his proposal and the Chairman eagerly agreed to meet him to discuss it. He felt these new proposals might persuade the National Health Service to reverse its decision. When he came off the phone Ken raised his arms and shouted, 'YES!' His frozen shoulder was completely free and has remained so ever since.

As I write this the fight to save the hospital continues – the Government is now meeting the Trustees for discussions. There is a little postscript, however. Ken invited me to go round the hospital and I was delighted to do so. The whole area has a vibrant healing energy. As we walked through the grounds the clouds above us clearly formed into the shape of angels.

The angels even orchestrated the way in which I met Ken and heard the story of the hospital. He is a very powerful healer and was giving someone healing at the clinic where he works as a volunteer. At the end of the session she said that angels had surrounded her and taken her up to heaven in the most beautiful experience. She told him that she felt he should read one of my books and offered him a choice of two she had with her. He chose *A Little Light on Angels*.

The following day he visited a friend at her house and she remarked that the room was full of angels. He related the story of the previous day and remarked, 'I'd like to meet Diana.' His friend told him I was giving a talk near his home. He was able to come to it and invited me to see the hospital.

Sometimes angels give you physical objects to remind you they are there helping you.

Nina Dickerson was living in Italy with her husband. He had been under considerable stress and was very ill. Most of the friends who had been her support system had moved away and she felt alone and quite desperate.

The weather was sizzling hot and they both felt frazzled. Added to that, they were in the process of moving back to England and were collecting boxes in which to pack their belongings. One morning as Nina's husband picked up a carton and put it into the car to take home, she reached inside herself and asked for a sign for both of them.

They drove home and hurried into the cool of the house. Later her husband went to fetch the box from the car. 'Look,' he called to her. There in the bottom of the carton were two little china angels with golden wings. She knew it was the sign she had asked for and they still sit on her windowsill as a reminder.

When we call on the angels for help, they will some-times give us pictures or a vision to show us that they are supporting our choice.

> Teena was a lawyer who wanted to do something different. One morning she picked the angel card, Truth. That day she resigned from her job and in the evening she had a vivid vision as she was dancing.
>
> A butterfly flew to a block of gold and there went into a black hole where it stifled and was dying. Then she saw the butterfly free in nature, and taking pollen as it wanted. It was living in harmony and abundance. She knew the angels were supporting her decision for a new life.

If you ask a question with sincerity, the answer will be given to you. Your task is to keep open and receptive. It may come in a book, in something someone says, or through the radio or television. The answer may drop into your head or be revealed in a dream. In some way the angels will bring an answer to you.

I was in Cape Town running courses and spreading information about angels. This is what one of the partici-pants, Paulette, told my promoter after the course.

'I had been sitting on my bed meditating all after-noon. I had been feeling really low and kept repeating, "Why are there no answers? Why are there no answers?" Then a friend phoned and said, "Put on the radio." It was Diana talking about angels.

'I immediately phoned for tickets for the course and was told that it was full. Suddenly a very strong feeling came to me to go to the main booking agency and I drove there immediately. They had just had two tickets returned.'

Paulette added that she knew the angels had caused that to happen.

Watch out for the signals. Listen to the quiet voice of inspiration, hope and guidance from your angel. Then you will follow your life path without getting lost.

Service work

Think of someone in need of reassurance or who is in doubt or uncertainty. Direct the angels to give them a clear signal of their presence.

Also watch for signals for others and remind them of their significance.

CHAPTER FIVE

Feathers

Angels draw attention to their presence with little white feathers. Your angel would love you to be able to talk to him, to feel his presence and to be able to touch you. If they cannot get through they will present you with a little white feather just to let you know they have heard your longing to make contact.

Here is a letter typical of many I receive. 'Since attending your angel workshop I have developed a closer and more personal relationship with my angel. However, that night I went home determined that I would see my angel or that he would somehow reveal himself to me but nothing happened. I awoke the following morning feeling very disappointed and I thought, "Typical! You want me to live a spiritual life and you couldn't even leave me a feather!" and lo and behold just by my foot on the floor lay this little white feather.'

Often we want the angels to take our life challenges away from us. Though they cannot do this, they will remind us that they are there to hold us.

Margaret was an alternative therapist who passionately believed in natural healing methods where possible. When she discovered a lump in her breast, she was told by doctors that she must have it surgically removed. She tried every alternative and natural method that she could but the lump did not respond. With a heavy heart she decided eventually that she must have it removed. After she took the decision, she went to the hospital toilet and a little white feather fell from nowhere on to her shoulder.

Operations are major learning opportunities. They offer lessons in patience, acceptance and surrender, as well as allowing yourself to be cared for and the chance to experience dependence. Many find it easy to give, while being helpless necessitates receiving. Undergoing surgery is a time when you can learn who cares for you and how loved you are. During convalescence you are forced to rest, which you may not do at any other time. You learn about your own physical weakness and strength.

Margaret knew she was being told that this was the right way for her and that the angels would be with her.

Angels keep floating feathers down to us as signals. When I am walking, if I notice a little white feather on the ground, I will try to remember what I was thinking about. I know the angels are particularly drawing attention to whatever my thought was and blessing it.

With synchronicity, as I was writing this a friend phoned to tell me that when she left my house a few days earlier,

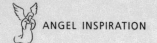

the motorway home was solid with traffic. She had an appointment and wanted to be on time.

As she reached the next junction she thought, 'Shall I come off here and cut across country?' No sooner had the thought crossed her mind than several little white feathers floated round her stationary car. Recognising this as strong guidance from her angels, she cut across country and was home in half an hour, in good time for her appointment.

Watch the signals from the angels and your life will run more smoothly.

During an evening talk on angels I mentioned that little white feathers were a sign that angels were present. The following day there was a message on my answerphone from someone who had been at the talk. He said that he and several others had gone to a café afterwards, where they discussed angels throughout their meal. When they stood up to leave, there, in the middle of the table, was a little white feather. It was a coloured wipe-down table and had been completely clear when they sat down. They were thrilled that angels had manifested their presence so immediately.

An angry man called in while I was doing a phone-in on the radio. His wife was longing for an angel signal. She had found a little white feather on the windowsill of their upstairs flat and was quite ecstatic. Her husband looked out of the window and saw that there was a dead bird on the lawn. He shouted down the line, 'The feather must have blown in when the window was open. If I hadn't seen that dead bird, she would have thought it was an angel!'

Now, angels do not necessarily manifest feathers from thin air. They have the power to do so, of course, but what a waste of energy! If there is a feather nearby, they will waft it into place.

As with everything, you are asked to use discrimination. If you walk by a lake where ducks and swans congregate, there will be plenty of feathers. These do not indicate that angels are there, though they may well be.

You can ask your angel to leave you a signal.

A publisher said to me that she had to make a tricky decision about a book. Everything had been turbulent and exceedingly difficult. So she told the angels that she needed help. She asked them to tell her what would happen if they decided to publish. When she had handed over the problem, she fell into her first deep sleep for days and in the morning a little white feather sat on her bedside table. Everything went smoothly with the publication.

The following story intrigued me.

Addie told me that she was really frightened about a situation in her life. She did not know what to do and felt very helpless and pressurised by other people. She listened to my angel tape and afterwards started to ask the angels for help. Two days later she woke in the night and saw lots of little angels round her bed. She was perplexed that some were black and others white but she felt quite safe and relaxed.

The following day she found a white feather on the stairs and knew the angels were signalling to her that the situation would resolve. She picked the feather up and, before she went to bed, she put it deep into the well of an ornament in her bedroom. She said to the angels, 'If you're telling me the truth about this, the feather will be gone in the morning.' The following morning the feather had disappeared completely. She searched everywhere but there was no sign of it.

Her difficult situation was totally sorted out that day.

Since then she has often woken in the night and seen her angels watching over her, making her feel secure and loved. Now she tells others about angels.

Addie's story contains some fascinating insights about faith. The angels knew she was ready to spread the word and signalled confirmation that they would help her situation by dematerialising the feather. The black and white angels also intrigued me. The colour in which an angel appears to you is significant. Significant means it contains a sign. Black and white together generally mean that there are two sides to a problem, a warning not to be too extreme. Black is the yin or feminine colour, which indicates mystery as well as darkness. White is yang or masculine, which indicates action as well as purity.

Service work

Whenever it is appropriate, mention the symbolism of little white feathers to those who are open to angels. It may change their lives.

CHAPTER SIX

Angel Touch

Whenever I am helping people to connect with their Guardian Angel, I ask them to expect their angel to make his presence felt in a physical way.

Some people literally feel a hand placed on them, so physically that they believe it is human and open their eyes. They are often shocked to find there is no one there.

At other times the sensation that your angel brings you is more subtle, the brush of a wing against your arm, a cool wind on your face, a waft of perfume, a sudden feeling of peace or love or a sense of being enfolded with wings. Often the moment is illusory and seconds later you are left wondering if you imagined it. I suggest you hold the moment in your heart because your angel has tried really hard to give you that experience to enable you to know of his presence.

I have often given healing to people who have been totally convinced that there were many healers physically touching them. In fact there was only myself and sometimes my hands were not actually on their body.

As I was writing these words a letter arrived from Linda Roberts, who had been to an evening talk I gave. She said, 'The most incredible part of the evening was being touched by an angel. I was a little sceptical that it would happen to me, but sure enough, I felt a stroke along my leg.'

Frederica Montague was sitting in meditation at a workshop. She felt the touch of an angel on her body and was so startled that she opened her eyes. There stood a huge white angel. It touched her all over her body and pulled out beliefs and problems from her physical, emotional, mental and spiritual bodies. She felt an incredible upliftment and it was the start of change in her life.

Angels will touch you in order to reassure you that all is well.

Sharon Lewis had an emergency caesarean, so her little girl, Aislin, was born eight weeks prematurely. She was in an incubator and both her lungs collapsed. She was critically ill and nearly died three times.

On the third occasion, Sharon was sitting by the incubator at 8.30 in the morning when she felt an invisible hand on her shoulder. She felt a great sense of relief and knew everything would be okay with her daughter. She knew she would live.

When her husband came in, she told him what had happened. He responded by saying, 'That's a really funny thing.' He related to her that he had gone into the kitchen for breakfast and Lewis, their four-year-old son was talking to someone, although no one was there.

'Who are you talking to?' he asked.

'Dad, I'm talking with the angels. Everything's going to be OK. She'll be fine.'

Her husband was considerably shocked, but little Aislin blossomed after that.

Angels will comfort you when you are in need of help.

> Heather wrote to me that her mother was having treatment for cancer. While she was sitting in the hospital, waiting for the results and feeling very upset and worried, she distinctly felt a hand laid on her shoulder, comforting her.

Do not think you have imagined it. Know that the angels are around you, empathising with you. They are longing to hold and help you. If you are open to their touch, you will feel it and it will heal and help you.

With the synchronicity I have come to expect from the angelic kingdom, as I was writing this chapter I received a letter from Robert Freeman, telling me of his glorious experience of being massaged by invisible angelic hands.

> Bob was tackling a DIY job in his house and sat down to look at what he was making. He wrote, 'I remember it vividly, the radio was on and there was a mess everywhere on the floor. As I looked at my work I felt a pair of hands on my back, massaging my spine, producing a feeling of absolute ecstasy in me. My first thoughts were, "Am I imagining this?" I was alone in the house and the chair I was sitting on had a bar on the back that would have interfered with a normal massage. The fingers were working themselves right into the spaces between my vertebrae, which would have been agonising if they had been physical fingers. I wanted to get up to switch the radio off because there was a song playing that I did not

like. But the feeling of ecstasy was so wonderful that I could not move.

'As I was wondering how long this could go on for, another set of hands started to massage the back of my skull, further increasing my ecstasy.

'At this point I could see movement in the form of white swirling vortices around me and then another set of hands were placed on my upper back and a wonderful sensation of heat came from them and penetrated my back. Then, as suddenly as it had started, it all stopped and I was left listening to the radio and looking at the mess on the floor and wondering, "Did that really happen"? But the hands felt as real as physical hands, though stronger and more gentle.'

When you call on an angel to enfold someone in their wings, they will do so. It can be a friend or a stranger. Whether the person is consciously aware of it or not, your request enables their Guardian Angel or an Angel of Love or Peace to step in and hold them tenderly.

All the people on the planet who are violent or controlling are acting from fear. Instead of condemning them, direct angels to hold them and rock them gently. At some level they will feel it. It is only when an abusive person feels safe that they can let go of their behaviour and open their hearts to higher possibilities. Through the angels you have the power to help them.

Service work
Open your heart and send angels to three people. Direct

the angels to enfold each of them in their wings and hold them tenderly.

Let one be someone you know really well.

Let the second one be a stranger.

Let the third one be a person who is misusing their position of power in some way.

Each time you do this your light will become brighter and more Beings of Light will surround you.

CHAPTER SEVEN

A Solution to Every Problem

There is a perfect solution for every relationship and every problem. The answers lie in the higher dimensions and often our human self cannot access them. In order to find the solution, we have to hand the situation over to God or his angels, then listen to and act on the prompting of our intuition.

Take the analogy of a child with a broken toy. If he asks Daddy to mend it, Daddy will be delighted to do so. He will take the toy and repair it. Then he will return it to the child complete. But if the child refuses to let go of the toy and wants it to be mended while he is still clutching it, it is impossible for Daddy to take it away and work on it.

Most of us insist on holding on to our worries and concerns. We hang on like grim death to our relationships and let problems go round and round in our heads. We agonise over each broken situation. Clearly the angelic realms cannot then do anything to help us. We remain stuck.

The angels are delighted to present us with a higher solution as soon as we are ready to pass the problem over to them. This means, of course, that we tell them about the situation and direct them to deal with it. Then we let go. *The only way of letting go is to stop worrying completely*. Worry forms the cord which pulls the problem back to us. Do not think about it. Do not talk about it. Handing a problem over completely is a test of faith.

Heather and her friends had to find student accommodation for their second year at university. They went out every night knocking on doors and explored every possible avenue. There was nothing available. At last they decided to meet every evening, light a candle and say a prayer for the house they needed.

A few days later a girl knocked on Heather's door and invited them to the Bible group she was starting up. They chatted and the stranger told Heather and her friends that she knew of a student house which was about to become vacant and gave them the address. She warned them to act quickly.

When she had gone, they went to the address she had given them. The house was two minutes away from their college. It was to be advertised the following day. The rent was much cheaper than they had expected. They moved in and stayed there happily for the next three years.

It transpired that the previous tenants had no clue as to who the girl was who had given them the address. No one had seen her around the college and no one had heard anything of the Bible group she said she was starting up.

Heather believed the angels had sent her in response to their prayers.

Even the most evolved and aware people sometimes forget to hand over to the angels.

My friend Grahame visited me one afternoon. He told me that he was going to have to move from his flat as he could no longer afford the rent. He was intending to phone the agents the following day to give them notice. I asked him what he could afford and he named a small amount that would just about rent a cupboard. I asked him if he had handed the problem to the angels and he said that he hadn't.

It is really helpful to have two or three people hold your vision with you. If you start to doubt, their strength maintains your faith. The same principle applies when you hand a problem over to the angels. So I offered to do it with Grahame and hold the focus.

He told the angels his problem and handed it over. I reminded him to listen to any intuitive flashes which came to him.

He phoned me a few days later and said that he had had an intuition to phone the landlady and tell her he would be leaving. He felt it was a courtesy as she had been very good to him. She asked him why he was leaving and he told her that he really could not afford the flat any longer. She asked what he could afford and he named this meagre sum.

She phoned him back half an hour later and said that she too had had financial difficulties when she was young. He had been a good tenant and she liked him. He could have the flat for eight months at that reduced rent and then they would talk again.

Grahame knows that if he had not handed his problem to the angels, he would have given notice to the agents the following day and would have been reduced to living in a tiny room. Angels literally work miracles.

A young mother was deeply anxious about her little girl who was being bullied at school. She worried continuously about the child. When you worry about your loved ones you pour a dark, heavy cloud of energy over them, which opens a sensitive person up to harm and ill health. It is about the most unhelpful thing anyone can do for those they love.

I suggested that she hand the problem over to the angels and then trust them to protect the child. She saw the sense of this, so she used her energy in putting golden light round her daughter.

Next time I saw her, the little girl looked so much happier. She told me that the bully had left the school.

Angels can find solutions that we would never think possible.

Service work
If there is a problem in your community or your country, tell the angels about it and ask them to find a perfect solution. Then let it go.

Join with others to hand world problems over to the angels. You must contract to stop worrying and let them deal with it.

CHAPTER EIGHT

Angels and Children

I have listened to many children who see angels. Without exception they talk with a simple clarity. Because they know they can trust me they explain what they see and hear in a matter-of-fact, unembarrassed way. It is wonderful to see their shining eyes as they talk of angels.

And yet so many parents tell me how difficult it is at school for their children, who are aware of the other dimensional worlds. They are afraid to say anything because others think they are weird and deride them. Of course, children who see angels are invariably sensitive and often find life in this gross world very difficult anyway. It is time for them to be treated with respect and reverence as the special children that they are.

> I was heartened recently when a thirteen-year-old told me that her teacher at school talked to the class about angels. The teacher asked if any of the children knew about them. Tiffany put her hand up, spoke about angels and said that she saw them.
>
> At the end of the lesson the kids crowded round her and were fascinated to hear what she had to say. Then several of them revealed that they too were aware of

angels and the spirit world but had never dared to admit it before.

I had the most fascinating conversation with Josie, who is seven. She has always seen angels. Her big eyes fastened seriously on to me as she told me that there were always angels around her, usually about four or five. She told me that her Guardian Angel changed colour all the time, depending on how she felt. Sometimes the colours were soft and at other times bright.

Her Guardian Angel was always talking to her, telling her what was the right thing to do, and mostly she did it. She said it was like thoughts coming at you from them.

The angels often help her at school. When I asked her how, she told me they help her to remember her seven times table and to find things.

'Do you ask them to do things?' I wanted to know.

'Yes. If the car isn't working, I say, "Please get the car going or I'll be late for school."'

'Does it work?' I persisted.

'Always.'

'What else do you ask for?'

'I ask them to help my little brother with his habits and to heal him when he hurts himself.'

Josie knows how people are feeling because she can see into them, so I was intrigued when she told me that the angels helped her to see other people's auras. She said, 'They make it clear, like tracking on a TV.'

She told me that angels can give you energy or they can give you Reiki or any other kind of healing. She ended by saying. 'Angels can do mostly anything.'

I felt really humbled talking to this wise child. She has a younger brother who has special needs and her mother felt she took advantage of Josie's good nature by asking her to look after him too often. One day the little girl said to her, 'Don't worry about me looking after him, Mum. I chose him to be my brother.'

At last, too, it is becoming safe for adults to talk about experiences they had with angels when they were children. Invariably these experiences are indelibly etched inside them.

At a lecture I gave in London a lady shared an experience she had when she was seven years old, when she was woken by a light during the night. It was getting brighter and brighter and she looked to see if her brother, who was in the next bed, was seeing the same thing. But he was fast asleep.

Out of the light emerged a pink angel with golden wings. The angel took her by the hand and out into the night, through the sky and to the stars. Then it brought her back to bed.

The experience was as real in the morning as it had been when it was occurring but of course, she added, she could not tell anyone.

Catherine attended a workshop in Southern Ireland and told us of her first angel experience when she was six years old. She was lying in bed, fast asleep, and was woken by an angel who appeared in front of her.

The angel showed her that her hands were healing hands. She held her hands up as she told us this to demonstrate how the angel had touched them. It was such a vivid and overpowering experience that she never forgot it and eventually became a healer.

It is such a delight that children are still open to the spirit world and can tell us what really occurs.

Pauline told me the following story. Her friend's five-year-old daughter, Annabel, and her husband were hijacked in their car. The mother was at home and learned about the hijacking from the police. Not un-naturally, she was completely distraught.

The police told her to stay at home as it could take hours for a resolution.

However, within a short time the door opened and in bounced their little girl. When her mother asked her, 'What happened?' she said, 'An angel with a sword came and stood on the car bonnet. The hijackers saw it and ran away.'

The hijackers may or may not have 'seen' the angel, but they certainly reacted. I hope it changed their lives.

Angels give us such a sense of peace and joy that their closeness affects us physically.

> After an angel workshop Monica connected all the time to her angels. She lost thirty pounds in weight. It just fell off her.
>
> The family was going through a difficult time and at New Year her children felt very down. She suggested that they all took part in a ceremony to invite the angels in. The whole family participated and the energy, which had been so heavy, became very light. After the ceremony, her eight-year-old daughter went to the toilet and came back with tears streaming down her face.
>
> 'Whatever's the matter?' her mother asked in concern.
>
> The child replied, 'I saw an angel. As I came out of the toilet there it was, as real as if it was solid. I followed it into the kitchen and it turned and smiled at me. Then it went.'
>
> Monica said her daughter's little face was so full of joy and tears that she could never have made it up.
>
> A friend of mine said to her little girl one night when she put her to bed, 'Just ask your angel to look after you.'
>
> Her daughter said, 'She always does, Mummy. Can't you see her? She's over there in the corner.'

Children are so close to the spirit world. Many of them are still open to fairies and angels. Those who no longer see them often sense them.

> Sheila Hurst attended an angel class. As she and her niece drove home they saw two silver-white lights in the shape of an angel swoop over the car. Sheila said they felt brilliant. When they arrived home she told her six-year-old grandson that she had seen angels and then she described them.
>
> The little boy said, 'I'm so happy I'm going to cry.' And a tear ran down his face.
>
> Whenever she returns from her angel class, he greets her with, 'Nana, have you seen the angels tonight?' and his little face is shining.

Service work

Whenever appropriate, talk to children about angels and how they can help you. Stay open to anything they wish to share with you about their experiences.

CHAPTER NINE

Human Angels

Angels appear to you in the form most acceptable to you. There are occasions when an angel will take on human form to help you in some way. At other times your angel will impress on a human to do or say whatever is necessary.

Nina Dickerson was starting to teach angel classes in her home. Her first class was on a freezing February day. The central heating boiler broke down and at eleven in the morning it was already bitterly cold in the house. Her husband was away and they lived in the middle of nowhere.

She felt really agitated about her class. How could she possibly hold it if there was no heating? To her relief, when she searched the Yellow Pages for a central heating engineer, she found one based not too far away. She called him and he agreed to come. Indeed, he arrived within half an hour.

She said, 'I don't know your name.'

He responded, 'I'm your Guardian Angel come to help.' He had the bluest eyes she had ever seen.

He fixed the boiler and when she asked if he would send the bill, he replied, 'Guardian Angels don't send bills.' Indeed, no bill ever arrived. When she looked in the Yellow Pages again, she could find no trace of his number.

That evening when the class finished, two of the participants drove away before the others. At eleven-thirty they phoned from home to say that two angels had manifested over the car. They both saw them. The second car left with two people in it. Again two angels appeared over the car and they both saw them.

If necessary, an angel will prompt a human to take on their angelic role.

This cutting from a Durban newspaper really made me smile. It was about a lady who had to go to a funeral in a notorious part of Durban. She parked her car behind a taxi and was about to leave it when the driver got out and advised her not to park there as the bad people in that area would surely steal her car.

She replied flippantly that it would be fine as the angels would look after it.

She then went off to the funeral, returning some time later to find the taxi driver still there. He said to her, 'Madam, I waited for the angels, but the Lord did not send any to your car. So I had to stay here and wait for you because I saw people who wanted your car. Now, I can go, madam.'

And here is an example of an angel whispering a message to be passed on to a stranger.

> Terri Myers wrote to me about her wonderful dog, Jupiter, who is nearly thirteen but still in good form. 'He's a medium-sized mongrel and the best-natured dog in the Universe, apart from his dislike of Alsatians,' she wrote. 'When he was young and vigorous, he would make this perfectly clear and there were some unhappy encounters. Now that he is too old to hold his own against a big dog, I have to be circumspect about whom he meets.'
>
> She was taking Jupiter for his evening walk recently when a lady she had never seen before stopped her and said, 'I'd be careful if I were you. There's an Alsatian off the lead up the road.' Terri was dumbstruck, thanked her profusely, turned around and walked swiftly the other way.
>
> She is sure that the lady was inspired by the angels to warn her.

An angel will occasionally take on human form when you need urgent medical assistance.

> Jan wrote to me of her experience. She and her friend Ken were walking down a steep slope when he tripped and fell. She could see from his face that he was in considerable pain.
>
> It transpired that Ken had broken his left shoulder badly and sprained his ankle. There was no way she

could move him on her own. It was dusk on a cold February day and they had not seen a soul during their walk. At that moment a man walked towards them and asked if he could be of assistance. He said he had done first aid. Together they helped her injured friend to a main road and the stranger looked after him while she fetched her car to take him to hospital.

Jan wrote, 'This man had such an air of calmness about him and was so gentle and kind to Ken that I felt he was heaven sent. He was such a nice man and to this day I have always thought of him as an angel.'

She added that it was one of those occurrences that you never forget.

Mary Davies had a similar experience when she and her husband were on holiday in Greece. They had hired scooters and often visited a distant beach which was completely isolated. It was invariably deserted.

One day, as they neared the beach, Mary skidded, went over the handlebars, cut her cheek and grazed herself badly. With the help of her husband, she hobbled to the sea to wash her cuts. When they turned around there, under an overhang, sat a woman all alone. She called out, 'Can I help?' She had a huge bag containing a complete medical kit. The stranger patched Mary up and it was only when they returned to their hotel that she thought, 'How did she get there without transport? Who was she? Why did she have a full medical kit with her?'

I would like to add one more human angel story that I have always remembered, partly because of the light on the face of the girl who told us this at a workshop.

When this girl was a student she was feeling very low. She cried out to spirit for help and immediately a friend phoned and said, 'Come over to see me.'

She filled her car up with petrol but had an uneasy feeling something was wrong, so she asked the attendant to check it. He did so and confirmed it was fine and she set out on her journey.

In the middle of nowhere the car stopped. She sat there all alone and very frightened. Ten minutes later a car pulled up next to her with two men in it. One of them got out. He said, 'We are angels sent from God and he wants you to know he loves you.' He got a can of petrol out of his boot and filled her car up. Then they drove off. Her car went perfectly.

She knew that God had sent them.

Treat everyone you meet as if they were an angel. You really may be entertaining angels unbewares.

Service work

Treat the next person you meet as if they were an angel. You will bring out the angelic qualities in them.

CHAPTER TEN

Miracles

A few years ago I had an excited and inspiring letter from someone whose sister had passed over and had started to communicate with her family through automatic writing. They sent me some of her letters, which described the joy and happiness on the other side of the veil. Most of all it talked of the beauty.

I was most struck, however, by the simple statement, 'There are angels. I have seen them. They are pure of heart and soul and only wish to help others.'

When angels come to help you they can make miracles happen.

Angels appear in many forms, sometimes as birds or butterflies or animals. They will show themselves in any way that is acceptable to you at that moment.

Melanie was in unimaginable emotional pain. Her father had shot himself. Soon after that her brother hanged himself. Her other brother overdosed. I can't even begin to comprehend what she was feeling. She sat by the river, staring into the water, at rock bottom.

Out of nowhere a white dove circled above her and dived into the water in front of her. As it rose again and circled above her, it took *all* her pain with it. It seemed

to say, 'I have taken the pain. Now get on with your life.'

From that moment she returned to her former happy self. And she knew the dove was a manifestation of an angelic force.

The following story touched me deeply. The lady who told it to me was in tears, as was most of the group.

She was looking after her grand-daughter, who was a toddler. She laid the child on the changing mat to put on a new nappy and went to get a fresh nappy from the closet. When she turned round the child had disappeared. She ran round the house and could not find her. Then to her horror she discovered that the back door was open.

Screaming to her daughter, she ran down the garden path and there was the toddler lying face down in the swimming pool. They got her out but she was not breathing. Her daughter phoned for an ambulance while she gave mouth-to-mouth resuscitation. There was no response.

A huge angel appeared beside her and told her not to give up.

When the police arrived they said, 'You're wasting your time. The baby's dead.' She carried on giving mouth-to-mouth anyway. The ambulance men came and also said, 'She's dead. Just let her go.'

All the time the angel was saying, 'Carry on. Get her

to hospital.' They tried to take the 'dead' child from her but she refused and insisted on continuing the resuscitation in the ambulance. The angel sat with them in the ambulance, encouraging her to continue and telling her that her grandchild would be alright.

The baby was treated in hospital and made a full recovery, with no hint of brain damage.

To me that is the most beautiful miracle.

Many people have talked to me of a presence surrounding them at a time of danger and helping them through.

Sam was a businessman whose hobby was to fly his glider. One day he was floating through the air, quite near the mountains, when a sudden mist engulfed him. He moved through it blind, fearing that he was getting inexorably closer to the mountains. Suddenly he felt a presence surrounding him. He knew that whatever happened he would be alright.

The glider hit the mountainside and was scattered in a million pieces. He was placed gently on a rock, totally unhurt. Again, the experience changed his life.

I was doing a radio phone-in about angels from my local studio. Naturally you could hear it in the reception area outside. A young man was waiting there to be a guest on another programme and was listening. He told the receptionist that an angel had helped him but he had

never told anyone about it. In the interval she brought him into the studio and he told the following story.

> He had been in the mountains on a mission. Unexpectedly a freezing, thick mist had fallen and he could not see his hand in front of his face. He could not leave the spot as it was too dangerous to try to move. In the mist he would never find his way back to his hotel and he had no idea what he would do as night was falling. All of a sudden a comforting hand touched his shoulder and an invisible being led him through the mist and down the mountain to safety.
>
> Later he learned that his granny, though she had no idea what he was doing or where he was, had sensed he was in danger and asked an angel to help him. Her intercession probably saved his life.

When coincidences, synchronicities and miracles start to happen in your life, you know that the angels are with you.

Service work
Watch for the coincidences, synchronicities and miracles in your life and that of others. Then point them out to people. Make people aware that the higher forces are orchestrating these.

Send angels to help all kinds of situations and miracles can happen.

CHAPTER ELEVEN

Angels Singing

Angels love to sing. That is why we refer to choirs of angels. And they really do play harps and trumpets. When you make a change in your life for the better, angels are celebrating your victory by trumpeting it into the heavens. When you raise your consciousness in meditation or in your life, the heavenly choirs maintain your vibration with sound.

A few years ago my daughter Dawn came to stay with me. She got up in the night to go to the bathroom and as she passed my bedroom she heard music coming from my room. In her half-asleep state she thought, 'That's angels singing.' On the way back from the bathroom she still heard this most beautiful sound. As she paused to listen she just knew it was the angels singing. Then she started to rationalise. 'It can't be. Mum must be playing an angel tape but it doesn't sound like a tape.' At that point she realised that my light was out and it was four o'clock in the morning.

The following day she talked about the beautiful angelic singing she had heard. Then she started to say, 'Well, perhaps I imagined it.' So I asked my guide, Kumeka. He roared with laughter and said, 'Of course

the angels were singing over you in bed. *If only you knew how often they do this.'*

I felt amazed and overjoyed. We are so cared for and nurtured by the angels.

Amanda Foster came to a workshop the day after her mother's funeral. She looked calm and composed and told me it was the angels who gave her the strength to be there. As her mother was dying she continuously asked the angels for strength for her and for the whole family.

Her sister did not really believe in angels until the occasion when she heard an angelic orchestra in the middle of the night. She could hear many different instruments playing the most incredibly beautiful music. Eventually she got out of bed and looked out of the window into the street in case there was something out there. As she rose out of bed the orchestra stopped playing. When she got back in again it started again. Then she felt a purple whoosh across her vision and all the pain of her mother's death was taken away. She felt wonderful.

Furthermore, Amanda told me, the whole family felt very strong and held by the angels.

The sound of angels singing heals and purifies.

When Larissa Johnson was nine or ten years old she had a very nasty dose of flu and was extremely ill. As she lay on the sofa with a high temperature she heard an angelic choir in the room. There were millions of angelic voices from the lowest base up to the highest soprano. She was scared and simply could not move as the angel choir sang over her.

Gradually the singing faded away until just one soprano remained. As soon as her voice also faded, Larissa's temperature was gone and she was completely well. She walked out of the lounge and said 'Hi' to her mother, who could not believe such a miracle could occur.

Very often the angels sing over you for the sheer joy of doing so.

A young lady, whose face beamed with light, shared her experience with me. She was asleep in her basement flat and was woken by the sun pouring in on to her. Then she realised that the sun never penetrated the basement. It was a beam of divine golden light and as she bathed in it, she could hear angels singing all round her.

Remember that you can invite the choirs of angels to sing over you at night. Then you will be bathed in their healing, purifying, joy filled sounds while you sleep.

Service work
Direct the heavenly choirs to sing over people in need or over hospitals.

Call them in to play peace music on their harps in places of war and conflict.

CHAPTER TWELVE

Angels of Sound

When asked to do so, the magnificent angels of sound will use your voice to heal, calm, purify or help you or others. If you sing, hum, chant, intone or play an instrument, they take the vibrations they need from your music and use them for heavenly purposes.

My daughter Lauren runs voice and toning classes. She always works with the angelic forces and the energy raised is truly special. The sound for the heart centre is 'Ah' and she taught me this beautiful way of opening the heart and bringing in the angelic forces.

If you are alone, gently rub the centre of your chest, which is your heart centre, while asking the angels to open your heart. Then raise both arms high while chanting 'Ah'. Smile and throw your head back as you do this.

It is even better if a group of you can hold hands and invite the angels to join you. Then all raise your arms high, chanting 'Ah'. Do this three times. When there are enough people, it sounds like singing in a cathedral.

An angelic sound bath is a wonderful way to connect with angelic energy. One person stands in the centre of a circle or sits against a wall. Simply ask the angels to use the vibration of your voice to give this person whatever they need. Then everyone hums or sounds the ohm to them. It feels magical with a group. Of course, just two people can also do this for each other, if necessary.

It is even more effective to chant or sing someone's name lovingly to them and direct the angels of sound to use your voice to bring healing. You chose your name before you were born and telepathically imparted it to your parents, so that they would name you accordingly. The vibration of your name calls your soul's lessons to you every time it is sounded. If it was said angrily or critically to you when you were a child you may have taken on the message that your soul's mission was difficult. In that case you will make life difficult for yourself.

Hearing your name sung lovingly by humans and angels is a life-enhancing and empowering experience.

On one occasion when I was facilitating a large angel workshop in Dublin I was unexpectedly prompted by the angels to invite good singers on to the platform. I was amazed at the response – suddenly there was a rush for the stage and it was full! I believe the angels called every one of those people.

Then I asked the singers to open up as channels so that the angels could sing through them. They would receive direct light from the angels and would then bathe the remainder of the audience in an angelic sound bath.

They decided to sing 'Amazing Grace'. As they sang, most gloriously, they were washed in radiant golden light and could feel the angels singing through them. I sat in the audience and received that energy. It was a most remarkable and memorable experience.

Since that time I have been asked two or three times by the angels to repeat this. It is never planned so it is a sudden surprise. And it is always fabulous. So whenever you sing, ask the angels to sing with you and through you.

You can ask the Angels of Sound to help you in many ways. Sound the ohm while you focus on one of your dreams or visions and call on the angels to energise it.

There is always a powerful response when you invoke Archangel Michael to dissolve cords which bind you to someone or something. If you intone for release while you picture the cords and call on Archangel Michael to dissolve them, it is very effective.

A wonderful way to heal your inner child is to ask the angels to enfold him or her. As you sense or visualise this, lovingly sing the child's name. Angelic love will flow into your inner child and free it.

Here is one of Lauren's meditations, where you connect with the angels of sound and the Archangels for healing. It is beautiful to do alone or in a group.

Lauren's Angel Meditation

1. Light a candle and then sit comfortably with your back straight and supported if necessary.
2. Relax for a few minutes as you watch the candle flame flickering.
3. Softly chant AUM three times and feel the resonance of this ancient mantra flowing round your body.
4. Close your eyes and see the flame in your mind's eye. Carry it down to your heart and let the flame of the

candle light the spiritual flame in your own heart.

5. Feel your heart sing with joy.

6. Very softly and gently call in your angels with an OOO sound. See them with you, adding their own laughter and strength to the flame in your heart. Let them add their sound to yours.

7. Be aware of them smiling at you as they acknowledge and thank you for asking them to help. They are around you and ready to work with you.

8. Call on Archangel Michael for protection, and Archangel Jophiel to give you wisdom and illuminate your heart and mind.

9. Ask the angels to sing with you to open up your heart to unconditional love. As you tone an AAAAH sound, feel your heart expand and see the pink ray of love pouring into it from the angels, which surround you. Let this love lift you and release you.

10. The light and love which are within you and surround you give you immense power to work with the light of the angels for healing. You can choose where to direct this light. In your mind's eye, see the situation, pattern or person you would like to send light to. See Archangel Michael and Jophiel on either side of this person or situation, encasing it in a ball of brilliant golden light.

11. Ask to be a channel for the angels to sing through and open up your throat centre with a gentle 'Eye' tone. Invoke the angels to sing through you and allow this sound to change as they do so. Let yourself be guided and know that whatever sound comes through you will be perfect. Visualise the situation changing as it receives and absorbs the healing sounds.

12. When your work is complete, mentally disconnect from the situation, person or pattern that you have been healing. Focus again on your angels beside you. Thank them for their help and listen for any further guidance they may have for you.

13. Make sure you are grounded. See the cords going from your feet, deep into Mother Earth, and feel her own energy coming up to meet yours, supporting and grounding you.

14. Open your eyes and focus on the candle flame again. Feel the flame of joy in your heart. Finally blow out the candle and dedicate its light to the person, pattern or situation you have been working on.

Service work

Lovingly sing the name of someone in need and ask the angels to enfold that person. It is particularly helpful to do this for leaders of repressive or violent regimes. It offers them the possibility of opening their hearts to change.

Focus on a negative place which is in need of clearing. Hum or tone and direct the angels to work with your sounds to transmute the low energy there.

CHAPTER THIRTEEN

While You Sleep

If you are not listening to the constant whispers of your angels guiding you and endeavouring to keep you safe, they will meet with your spirit guides and discuss what is the best way to help you. Together they will try to persuade you to change what you are doing.

Angels are particularly helping you when you are asleep at night.

> Tamara was aware that she had a blockage of anger in her heart centre. After a workshop she felt emotionally exhausted and in pain, which she recognised as an important sign that things were happening. She wrote, 'I went to sleep and while I was sleeping I began to experience severe chest pains. A Presence spoke to me in my sleep (I saw nothing) and told me that I could continue to sleep, allowing myself to breathe easy and that there was no need to worry, I was alright.'
>
> She felt no fear and sensed a great release in her upper chest as the pressure of anger was freed.

We all hold anger, fear, guilt, jealousy, hurt and other damaging emotions. You can always ask your Guardian Angel to help you release emotional blockages during

sleep, before they inevitably build up into physical problems.

Sherren Mayes came to interview me and told me the following story. She used to drive far too fast and was clearly in danger. One night as she lay asleep a cluster of luminous beings gathered in the corner of her room. They were mostly men. They were discussing her driving and debating it quite seriously.

At last she had had enough. She sat up, saying petulantly, 'OK! OK! I won't drive more than seventy miles an hour!' This action woke her and it was only then that she became aware of who the beings were.

The following day she had to drive to Devon to see her brother. Fortunately she clearly remembered her agreement of the night before and was driving very steadily. As she approached Devon a dreadful storm hit suddenly. Torrential rain lashed down and the wind buffeted the car. She had to slow right down to get through it. At one point she had to divert as an uprooted tree blocked the road. One of her headlights was ripped off and her brother said that she must have been mad to drive in it at all. If she had been travelling at her normal fast pace when the storm hit, she would have been in real danger.

Light beings are androgynous, totally beyond sexuality. So it is interesting that they chose to appear to Sherren as male. I believe this is because in our society we still invest authority in the masculine. If the light beings had been bringing compassion and tender healing,

they would possibly have chosen to present th
as female forms.

I wonder if the cluster of luminous beings we
guides and angels meeting to consult about her. It is
humbling to think that there are so many loving light
beings assigned to help us. They do particularly try
to get through to us at night when our whirling
thoughts do not block them, so it is always helpful to
relax your mind before sleep and remind yourself to be
receptive.

You are on assignment to your Earth mission twenty-
four hours a day and a very important part of this is
during your sleep time, when your spirits travel out of
your body. Depending on your consciousness your spirit
will go to lower or higher realms. If you have night-
mares you have visited the lower astral regions. When
your thoughts and actions are predominantly about love,
kindness, cooperation and the higher worlds, you will
visit the angelic kingdoms.

You may also go to the halls of learning or wisdom,
the temples of the Ascended Masters or to serve in
healing establishments in the inner planes.

Before you go to sleep, spend a few moments in quiet
contemplation and gratitude for the day. Then ask that
you be taken to where you want to go. If you particularly want to receive guidance, direct your spirit to visit
Archangel Gabriel's spiritual retreat at Mount Shasta. If
you wish to learn more about music or symbols or archi-
tecture, direct your spirit to the appropriate temple of
instruction. If you wish to become a purer channel for
healing, ask to serve with the great healing masters and

angels. At some level you will bring back what you need into your physical life.

Service work

Before you go to sleep, ask that your spirit go to help others. You can specify who you want to help or comfort or where you wish to go.

Ask that you be totally protected.

Direct the angels to accompany you and help you.

Passing Over

Sometimes people do not pass into the light when they die. In that case they hang around in the astral planes, often very frightened and angry, and they hook onto people they knew on Earth.

Joanna told me of her terrible panics and fear of dying. After much talking we established that it started when her mother had died ten years ago. It was only then that I became aware that her mother had not passed over properly and was linked in to her daughter. She was sending her own fear and panic down to Joanna.

When we called on the angels for help they immediately came in and severed the link with the mother. We prayed for a proper passing for the mother and asked Joanna's grandmother and the angels to help. At once the mother's mother, who was in spirit, appeared and Joanna's mother was relieved and delighted to be reunited with her. The angels surrounded them and helped her to move to the Light.

Joanna's panics stopped immediately.

We view life from a limited and often jaundiced perspective when we are in a body. When we expand into our spiritual body, everything appears very different.

Pam Pelling came from a family where little affection was demonstrated. She could never remember her mother kissing her. Like most people, she translated this as meaning she was not loved.

Twenty-six years ago she was very ill in hospital, so poorly that she was lying in an oxygen tent. Pam was deeply unconscious and the doctors said that she would not survive the night.

During the night she had an out-of-body experience. She saw her mother, father and husband around the bed with a nurse. She became aware of the love her mother really had for her, which she was unable to express.

Then suddenly she felt an angel push her right back into her body and she recovered. However, life appeared different from then on.

Many people believe that when a loved one dies they are lost to them for ever. Of course, this is not true. Your loved one is very much alive and has moved to a different frequency, which is usually invisible to you. This is why you can often connect in dreams, when your spirits can meet.

After her husband died, Frances frequently dreamt that he was dead. When she connected with the angels she dreamt he was alive and in the room. It was very real.

She realized that death as we understand it is an illusion. Once you die, you are very well, free of your physical body, working in the spiritual realms.

It is never too late to forgive another. It is never too late for a spiritual experience or to connect with your angel.

Petra's mother was dying and the family was waiting at the bedside for her to pass. Suddenly the old lady muttered through tight lips, 'I'll never forgive her.'

Petra said, 'Mummy, have you got someone to forgive?'

Her mother opened her eyes and looked at her.

Petra urged softly, 'Forgive her now.'

The dying woman murmured the Lord's Prayer and then relaxed into the pillows. She had never been a believer but just before she died her eyes lit up as she met her angel. She told the family that her angel's name was Maria. She also saw cherubs dancing round her bed.

A friend of mine, Paula, was talking to a lady whose horse was sick. She offered to give Reiki healing to the horse and said that she usually works with Reiki and angels. The lady told her this story, which she had never previously told anyone.

Paula was woken at 5 a.m. by a light and opened her eyes. A radiant angel stood there and told her he was her father's angel. The angel said that he had died but he was alright. Paula felt calm and warm, held by the light.

When the angel had gone she woke her husband and told him what had happened but he said it was a

---

hallucination, that she was not to be silly and to go back to sleep. At seven o'clock the phone rang and it was a message to say that her father had died at 5 a.m. She never mentioned the angel again until Paula talked openly to her.

The following is one of my very favourite stories, told to me by Irene. It always touches my heart when I think of it.

Irene told me of a particularly difficult time for her family when her father-in-law died two days before Irene's baby was born. He husband had gone to his funeral and she was lying in bed in a room on her own in the hospital.

Suddenly a light appeared at the window and came through it. It was an angel, who said, 'Don't worry. We've not come to harm you. We've just come to see the baby.'

The light divided in two. She could feel the presence of the angel and another person, who went and enveloped the crib. Then they merged and gently withdrew.

Irene realized that the baby's grandfather had been brought to visit him.

Although the following is not strictly an angel story, it does illustrate the freedom we have after death. Rose told me that her father died of lung cancer. She simply could not cope with seeing him dying and absented herself. However, after he died she just had to see him to say she was sorry she was not there for him at the end. She went to the room where he was laid out.

He was sitting in a chair by his body, wearing a bright-coloured dressing-gown. He was so real that she was able to touch him and kiss him goodbye. He said to her, 'This is wonderful. It is so nice where I am. It is joy and there is no fear.'

Service work
Pray for angels to help those who have passed over. They will receive and appreciate angelic assistance.

CHAPTER FIFTEEN

The Angelic Hierarchy

There are two parallel evolutionary spirals. One is the human line, which is said to come from the mind of God. This evolves as follows:

Mineral kingdom
Plant kingdom
Animal kingdom
Human kingdom
Ascended Master
Ascended Master levels to Source

Each of these kingdoms is contained within a frequency band. Humans are multi-dimensional and span the frequency bands.

The mineral kingdom operates in the first dimension. It experiences and evolves in this range. This is where new ideas root.

The plant kingdom, which needs light in order to grow, evolves within the frequency of the second dimension. Here there is an opening to spiritual information and knowledge.

Animals and those humans who only believe in a physical reality operate within the range of the third dimensional frequency. Right now we are in an incredible time of change. Enough people on Earth have opened their hearts and raised their consciousness to enable the planet itself to raise its frequency. Because of this, Earth has now shifted into the fourth dimension. You are all affected by this higher vibration. You blow a fuse if you put too high a current through an electrical appliance. Life seems uncomfortable if you are not ready for the higher current passing through you. Those humans who are still mainly living at the lower frequency feel very shaken up indeed.

People who are in the fourth dimension are beginning to open their heart chakras, remember past lives and expand their spiritual awareness.

When they pass over, some, who are motivated by love, choose to train in the inner planes as guides for those still on Earth. Higher guides come from even higher dimensions to help us.

Your aim while on Earth is to become a fifth-dimensional human and step on to the Ascension Pathway. You will then be a team leader, leading others on to the path of light. You may evolve to become an Ascended Master, one who has mastered the lessons offered on this planet. Then you can create heaven on Earth.

After death you continue to evolve and experience through the higher dimensions until you are ready to return to the Godhead.

The second evolutionary line comes from the heart of God and is as follows:

The elemental kingdom
Angels (Guardian Angels are the least evolved)
Archangels

Principalities
Powers
Virtues
Dominions
Thrones
Cherubim
Seraphim

The elemental kingdom contains fairies, gnomes, goblins, elves, undines, mermaids and so on. They are called elementals because they are made up of one element only and are ethereal, of the ethers, and therefore invisible to us.

Their task is to look after the nature kingdom. Air elementals, such as fairies, tend the flowers, mixing the colours and encouraging them to bloom and be fragrant. Earth elementals such as gnomes and goblins and many other tiny creatures work with crystals, sand, soil and jewels. Water elementals are the mermaids, undines and others who regulate the waters and help the creatures who live in them. Fire elementals are called salamanders and they tend the flames.

Elementals respond to the thoughts of humans. Fairies cooperate when we care for and nurture our garden, without pesticides. Salamanders, for instance, can get out of control, and therefore fire gets out of control when humans are angry.

When we bulldoze land, chop down bushes and trees, pollute the air and water and dynamite the land, the elementals who are looking after and creating the natural world we rely on cannot do their job. They are in despair for they cannot even grow and evolve.

In places where they are honoured and respected, humans and elementals co-create abundance in the nature kingdom.

The lowest rank of angel are those delegated to look after humans and keep our personal records for us. These are our Guardian Angels and there are millions of other angels being directed to our planet now to help with the consequences of the dimensional shift which has taken place.

The Archangels serve in a cosmic capacity and have responsibility for the angels and Guardian Angels on Earth.

Higher-ranking than the Archangels are the Principalities, Luminous Ones in charge of towns, cities, sacred sites, countries, nations, big corporations, big schools and any large venture.

In this time, when big is considered better, the Principalities have to work very hard. They hold in their hearts the divine perfect blueprint for each project or town.

Many hospitals are more like impersonal cities than gentle, nurturing places where you can be restored to health. A Principality will be overseeing the organisation of such a place. If you feel that aspects need to be looked at or changed, in your quiet time tell the Principality in charge of that hospital how you feel. Send up a clear vision that the place evolve for the best health and healing of the people using it.

The same applies to vast educational establishments, huge shopping arcades, enormous ships and business empires.

You may say, 'Why don't they use their power to

change things?' It is rather like a teacher putting on a play with a group of children. The teacher has the concept of a perfect production but can only do with the children what they are ready for. The Principalities hold the vision for the evolution of Earth but can only take us as fast as we are willing to go.

Like all angels, the Principalities can use the energy of your vision for the highest good. They can use the power of your thoughts to weave higher ideals into the world plan.

Service work

Send thoughts of peace, love and gratitude to the elementals of the nature kingdoms. Send your visions of beautiful cities, caring hospitals, education establishments conducive to learning and wisdom, fair governments and cooperative ventures to the Principalities so that they can create a better world.

Archangels

and

The Higher Hierarchy

CHAPTER SIXTEEN

The Higher Hierarchy

The second tier of the angelic hierarchy rises through the Powers, Virtues, Dominions, Thrones and Cherubim to the Seraphim.

The Powers include the mighty Lords of Karma and the Angels of Death and Birth.

The Lords of Karma are those Great Ones who preside over the collective and individual Akashic records of humanity. They keep the collective history of the planet and guard the conscience of humanity.

Karma is the just return to you of all you have sent out. Your life reflects it back to you. Even your body is your karma. It is your feedback system.

There are seven members on the board, each representing one of the rays. They are:

Ray 1	The Great Divine Director
Ray 2	The Goddess of Liberty
Ray 3	Lady Nada
Ray 4	Pallas Athena, The Goddess of Truth
Ray 5	Elohim Vista
Ray 6	Kwan Yin, Goddess of Mercy
Ray 7	Portia, the spokesperson for the Karmic Board, the Goddess of Justice

The Great Divine Director represents the first ray of will, power and drive. He is the Great Cosmic Being, who is the authority of the Cosmic Law to this planet. For more than 200,000 years He has been directing cosmic light rays to prevent humanity from destroying itself and the natural world. He was St Germain's Master.

The Goddess of Liberty represents the second ray of love and wisdom. She carries the energy of freedom through equality for humanity.

Lady Nada represents the third ray of love and active intelligence. She is often depicted in pink, the colour of Archangel Chamuel, the Angel of the Heart. When you act with purity of intention and aim high, she is supporting you. In her incarnations in the Mystery Schools of Atlantis, Egypt and Peru, her role was to encourage and lead others forward.

Pallas Athena represents the fourth ray of harmony through conflict. She was once the high priestess in Atlantis. She was also the favourite daughter of Zeus and Queen Nefertiti. She carries the divine quality of integrity for Earth and helps all those who are bringing truth forward.

Elohim Vista represents the fifth ray of research and the concrete mind. She is also representing, on the Karmic Board, the Elohim, the creator Gods. They are those who were created by the will of God in order to help Him build the form of the Universe. They work through the Archangels in this plane. Elohim means 'all that God is'.

Kwan Yin represents the sixth ray of devotion and idealism. She is known as the Goddess of Mercy and Compassion and is the Eastern equivalent of Mother Mary. She reintroduced Magnified Healing to Earth in response to our needs. Kwan Yin is said to have had a 1,000 year incarnation in China, where she was a Goddess. She is the Master in charge of birth and healing. She works with the threefold flame of gold for wisdom, pink for love and blue for power.

Lady Portia represents the seventh ray of ceremonial order and magic. She is the spokesperson for the Karmic Board, the Goddess of Justice. She holds the balance of mercy and judgement and helps those who want to balance heart and head. She frequently offers grace.

Divine dispensations have now been granted transmuting the karma of many, but not all, countries. This has happened at a causal level, though it still has to percolate down into the mental, emotional and physical levels. Much individual karma has also been transmuted thanks to the grace of the Lords of Karma. Many people are still unnecessarily paying off karmic debts, which have been cancelled.

You no longer have to carry the burden of past life mistakes and miscreations unless you insist on doing so! It is always worth respectfully approaching the Lords of Karma in meditation and asking if your debts have been or can be cancelled. Very often, all or a portion of karma is released, freeing your life path.

During a residential workshop, in meditation, we visited the Lords of Karma and Bob Freeman was given this information. The Lords of Karma want to release all karmic debt but this would cause more damage than good. Karma is adjustment. It is also compassion for it prevents souls from getting into deeper trouble. It is a backup system. Those who think that there is no spiritual meaning to life would do damage if they were not restricted. Bob was told that the more we are attuned to the possibility that there is something other than the physical, the more quickly all karmic debt dissolves.

The Lords of Karma told him that they wanted karmic debt to be released as quickly as possible so that Earth could be purified in order to accelerate the anchoring of the next five rays into the planet.

The Angel of Death then said to Bob, 'I want to be made redundant, for people to live as long as they want and then to ascend.' He was told the spiritual hierarchy wants us all to ascend even more than we want to. They ask us to inspire those we come across to aspire to ascension.

These are end times now. We must end our old way of being and tie up all loose ends in our lives, so that our planet can ascend to a higher frequency. We need urgently to clear the karma of the planet. Because of this individuals are taking on the unresolved karma of their family and their country as well as parts of the collective karma.

A psychic told a friend of mine that her great-aunt had undertaken a life of isolation in order to learn self-sufficiency. Her great-aunt lived alone except for a female companion, as was usual in those days, and appeared to be contented, but apparently she had always felt very different and alone. In fact she had learnt less than a tenth of what she had undertaken to learn during that life. The psychic told my friend that she had agreed to take on the rest of her great-aunt's lesson of isolation and aloneness, which was her karma, to clear it for the family.

She visited the Lords of Karma in meditation and asked for the family debt to be cleared, and it was. She then felt much better.

During the same group meditation Andrea was told that her husband had picked up the mantle of his grand-mother's uncleared debt but he died before he was able to deal with it all. She loved her husband greatly and because he was the last of the family there was no one else to take it on. So she had picked the debt up for him.

When we visited the Lords of Karma Andrea was disappointed that she could not see or hear anything. However, when she asked for her own family karma as well as her husband's to be released, she sensed them querying it. Why was she carrying her husband's family karma? It was as if they were saying, 'Do you really want to do this?' As they looked into it and she waited for a response from them, she felt a great love for her husband and the love went back through his family. Then she felt it all being released.

My guide told me that it was a very important act of service to meditate with others and ask for the karma of places to be released. Approach the Lords of Karma and, assuming your request is granted, direct armies of angels to help in the process, he instructed.

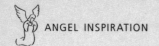

We did this with several hundred people in London, and millions of lost souls, those who had passed over but were stuck, those who had been aborted and those who were attached to Earth through drugs or alcohol, were freed to move into the Light. Also a vast cloud of negative thought forms and dark emotions was lifted from the city.

You have the power to do this, on your own or with friends. Ask the angels to protect and help you when you do this.

Beyond the Powers are **the Virtues,** who are sending huge beams of light to Earth to facilitate the changes in consciousness now taking place. As you work with them, there will be greater amounts of spiritual light available for us all.

The Dominions are the angelic order, which oversees the angelic hierarchy below them. They act as channels of mercy and help us to move into the spiritual realms.

The Thrones receive direct illumination from Source. They are transformers of divine wisdom into a level that humanity can accept. They look after and guard the planets, and Lady Gaia is in charge of Earth.

Cherubim are the Angels of Wisdom. They are guardians of the stars and the heavens.

Those highest in the angelic hierarchy are the **Seraphim,** whose essence is pure love. They surround the Godhead, constantly singing the praises of the Creator, and maintaining the vibration of creation. They direct the divine energy, which emanates from Source.

Service work

On your own or with friends, meditate and petition to approach the Lords of Karma. Decide on a place or nation you would like to help. Tell the Lords of Karma that you wish to direct your energy there. Visualise millions of angels lifting the darkness from that place or those people. If you wish to make this more powerful, ohm as you direct your energy into that area.

CHAPTER SEVENTEEN

The Archangels

The Archangels are above the angels in the hierarchy. There are millions of Archangels throughout the Universes. However, very few connect with us on Earth. These mighty beings from the Great Central Sun have great power and light and each has a masculine and a feminine aspect.

There are seven Archangels and their Archeia or twin flames, associated with the seven rays. They work in cooperation with the Great Masters of Shambhalla, who head each ray. These are:

Ray 1   Michael and Faith. Michael means 'Who is like God'

Ray 2   Jophiel and Christine. Jophiel means 'Beauty of God'

Ray 3   Chamuel and Charity. Chamuel means 'He who sees God'

Ray 4   Gabriel and Hope. Gabriel means 'God is my strength'

Ray 5   Raphael and Mary. Raphael means 'God has healed'

Ray 6   Uriel and Aurora. Uriel means 'Fire of God'

Ray 7   Zadkiel and Amethyst. Zadkiel means 'Righteousness of God'

Each Archangel is connected to a particular element. Your sun sign may indicate which Archangel you are aligned to.

Michael is fire	Aries, Leo, Sagittarius
Gabriel is water	Cancer, Scorpio, Pisces
Raphael is air	Gemini, Libra, Aquarius
Uriel is earth	Taurus, Virgo, Capricorn

When you invoke the seven Archangels, great light, joy and protection are conferred on you. One of the greatest and most powerful invocations is this.

I now invoke the mighty Archangel Michael to stand at my right-hand side. Please pour courage and strength into me and bring about positive results to my endeavours. Cut all my negative cords and attachments with your sword. Place your deep blue cloak of protection over me so that only that which is of the highest and purest light may enter my aura. Thank you.

Pause for a moment so that Archangel Michael can complete this work and communicate anything he wishes to you.

I now invoke the mighty Archangel Gabriel to stand at my left-hand side in his pure white ray. Pour your pure white energy into my aura and bring me guidance about my next step or my pathway. Please illuminate and activate the symbols of my life's mission now. Bring joy, grace, clarity, understanding, generosity and order into my life. Thank you.

Pause for a moment so that Archangel Gabriel can

83

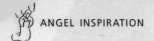

complete this work and communicate anything he wishes to you.

I now invoke the mighty Archangel Uriel to stand in front of me and fill my aura with his purple and gold ray of wisdom and peace. Soothe all conflict in my life and replace it with serenity, brotherhood and sisterhood. Please break my mental and emotional chains and free me from all my fears. Thank you.

Pause for a moment so that Archangel Uriel can complete this work and communicate anything he wishes to you.

I now invoke the mighty Archangel Raphael of the emerald ray to stand behind me. Please pour healing and abundance into me. Protect my journeys and impress me with justice, truth and vision. Thank you.

Pause for a moment so that Archangel Raphael can complete this work and can communicate anything he wishes to you.

I now invoke the mighty Archangel Chamuel of the pink ray to expand the flame of love in my heart. Please help me to find compassion and forgiveness for myself and for everyone I have ever harmed knowingly or un-knowingly. Open my heart now at a personal and cosmic level. Thank you.

Pause for a moment so that Archangel Chamuel can complete this work and can communicate anything he wishes to you.

I now invoke the mighty Archangel Jophiel to pour the

golden light of wisdom and illumination on to me through my crown centre. Let your wisdom light up and inspire my mind, helping me to learn and teach at the highest level. Please light up and activate now the symbols of wisdom I have accumulated throughout my lifetimes. Thank you.

Pause for a moment so that Archangel Jophiel can complete this work and can communicate with you if he wishes to.

I now invoke the mighty Archangel Zadkiel of the violet ray of mercy, joy and transmutation to pour the violet flame into my aura. Please release and dissolve all my negativity and replace it with joy, diplomacy and tolerance. Thank you.

Pause for a moment so that Archangel Zadkiel can complete this work and can communicate with you if he wishes to.

Your aura is now filled with the energy of the Archangels and you are connected to your mighty I AM presence. You are blessed.

In traditional Kabbalah there are ten Archangels. These are **Metatron, Ratziel, Tzaphkiel, Tzadkiel, Khamael, Michael, Auriel, Raphael, Gabriel, Sandalphon**.

Sandalphon is Archangel of the Earth who brings glory to the Kingdom. He is the steward who rules the kingdom, establishes peace and joy and brings the nature elements into harmony. The stability he offers brings us freedom.

Metatron represents the brilliance and glory of God and the judgement of the Divine throne, while Rachael, his twin flame, represents the power of the feminine. Metatron's name is said to mean 'One who occupies the throne next to the Divine throne'. Many sources believe him to have been the prophet Enoch. Metatron imparts knowledge of the higher dimensions to all those who are ready at a level they can understand.

Mighty as the Archangels are, they still appear to those who are ready.

Catherine Seiler has had many angelic encounters. A few years ago her husband's business was floundering and she was deeply unhappy. That evening a mighty angel appeared in front of her. He seemed as big as the whole Earth. She wrote; 'He picked me up and held me up in front of his beautiful face, and beamed so much love on me. He told me that he was Metatron.'

The following day she was sitting with her head in her hands in despair, feeling so alone and in a great deal of pain. Suddenly she heard a voice say, 'Child, you who gazed upon the face of Metatron, why are you in so much despair?'

She was startled and said, 'Pardon?'

Again the voice said, 'Child, who gazed upon the face of Metatron, why do you feel so much despair?'

She asked who was speaking. The voice answered, 'Mighty Metatron.'

Again she asked the same question and the same answer came again, 'Mighty Metatron.' Yet again she asked who was speaking. This time the answer came, 'I AM WHO I AM.' Then lovingly the voice told her not to worry or to be afraid, for so many beautiful and wonderful things were going to happen and she was not alone but very much loved.

She wrote: 'To tell the truth I was astonished that they would want to bother with me, but the love I felt and the reassurance I received was quite literally out of this world.'

Archangel Moroni appeared to Joseph Smith and led him to discover inscribed golden tablets, which became the Book of Mormon. They co-founded the Mormon religion.

Melchizedek was a high Archangel who took human form and founded the Order of Melchizedek, to teach spiritual truths and coordinate the work of the Christ on Earth and throughout the Universes. Jesus Christ was a high priest in the Order of Melchizedek.

As with all spiritual beings, you can invoke these Great Ones to work with you and empower your service.

Service work
Invoke the seven Archangels of the rays to surround and expand the consciousness of others, especially those in a position of influence in the world.

CHAPTER EIGHTEEN

Archangel Michael

The mighty Archangel Michael is the Angel of Courage, Strength and Protection.

If you invoke him, he will stand at your right-hand side, holding his sword and shield, ready to guard you. He will place his deep blue cloak round you for both physical and psychic protection.

He is a warrior Archangel, the commander-in-chief and stable ruler. He will give you initiative, willpower, drive and vitality to follow your path and complete tasks without effort or anxiety. He will help you develop leadership qualities and be strong, firm and focused enough to be successful.

His twin flame is Faith who, as her name suggests, confirms your confidence, or faith in yourself, so that you can accomplish your mission.

They are the Archangels of the first ray, and they work with El Moreya, the Master or Chohan of the red aspect of the first ray. Together they are bringing forward those with a strong sense of personal power, who can carry the sword of truth. Those who are closely connected to Archangel Michael are strong and powerful, whether they bring this through in business, via their writing, being part of the police or military, or in some other way.

Those who express the divine quality of this ray will be motivated, enthusiastic, strong and protective of those who need help. The lower expression of the first ray, which may need to be overcome, would be arrogance, the desire to control others, obstinacy and lack of feeling or tolerance.

If you are ever in danger, call on Michael. A lady I know was being psychically attacked by someone who felt rejected by her. He was sending her daggers of anger and darts of jealousy. This continued for some time and, as she was sensitive, she could feel the physical pain and sense of depletion. When she started to call on Archangel Michael to protect her with his cloak and shield, the pain and exhaustion vanished.

Michael will protect your property. Invoke him to look after your home at night or when you are away. I received this letter from Terri Myers, who had attended some of my workshops.

'My husband and I had decided not to insure the contents of our flat for financial reasons. However, I had asked Archangel Michael to guard the flat both internally and externally. I knew as I asked that this was done immediately, although I did not say this to anyone.

'At about the same time my nephew and I attended your Seventh Heaven workshop. Since then Daniel has opened psychically, sees and feels different energies. About a month ago, Daniel and I were returning home when he looked up, paled and said, "Terri, there is a big magenta angel with a sword in her hand and she is sitting on the roof." Of course, I knew at once that it was one of Michael's angels guarding our home.'

Susie Anthony was rescued from death on several occasions by no less than Archangel Michael himself. A crack cocaine addict, her first near death experience resulted from a seventy-two-day binge on a cocktail of class A drugs. As she died she felt her spirit leave her body and was approached by an immense shining pillar of royal sapphire blue light, which identified itself simply as 'Michael'. Later she discovered it was the Archangel.

In death Susie was cocooned in peace, love and compassion beyond human comprehension as she was gently guided through her life review. Michael revealed to her that her personality self was filled with such deep self-loathing and despair that no mere mortal could have reached her. Yet she had made a sacred life contract before being born to bring in great light to the darkness of Earth. She learnt that her soul carried enormous wisdom and healing power.

Her choice was to remain in the peace of the other side or to return and fulfil her contract on Earth, with new gifts and keys bestowed on her by Archangel Michael.

She returned and totally healed her physical body, which had been ravaged and destroyed by her addiction to drugs. Susie is writing a book about her awesome meetings with Archangel Michael.

Nora wrote to me after attending a workshop.

'I now have a sense of safety, which I seemed to lack over the past ten years or so. I feel this lovely atmosphere of being surrounded with care and love. I never did think that was possible. I live alone but I am no longer alone.' It is a unique feeling to be surrounded by the presence of angels in your daily life.

Nora confided in me that she had always had a terror of going to the dentist. She was forced, however, to make an appointment and felt very anxious indeed about going. This time she called on Archangel Michael for support. About five minutes before she reached the surgery she just 'knew' she was not alone. She wrote, 'Oh, the sense of peace and safety that suddenly surrounded me was indescribable.' This stayed with her until about ten minutes after leaving the surgery. The following week Archangel Michael returned when she visited the dentist for her second appointment and she had a repeat performance.

Archangel Michael's angels arrive as soon as they are needed. Whenever I visit South Africa I hear many tales of violence. Correspondingly I hear wonderful stories of angelic protection.

Gemma told me that she was alone in her home when five black men burst in and tied her up. In her area a lot of rapes and robberies were taking place and she was normally a very hysterical person, who panics easily.

However, as soon as the men burst in she was taken out of her body and above the scene. An angel held her and told her to be very calm and still. He said that as long as she remained calm everything would be alright. When she came back into her body and opened her eyes again she still felt held in that total peace. The men did not harm her.

> She lost all her material possessions but in her own words, 'Spiritually I gained everything.'
>
> Her whole concept of life was transformed by this angel experience.

You can ask Archangel Michael to protect those you love. His power will give them a sense of courage and security. If you ask him to place his deep blue cloak of protection around them, other people's negative energy will slide off them and leave them feeling more confident and stronger.

You can do this for acquaintances and strangers if you wish to serve humanity by bringing more of Michael's light into the planet.

Service work

Ask Archangel Michael to place his deep blue cloak of protection around you.

Then direct him to place his deep blue cloak of protection around people and places, known and unknown to you. Your prayers may be the intercession needed to save someone from harm.

CHAPTER NINETEEN

Michael's Angels of Protection

The power of the angels is awesome. They can literally dematerialise and rematerialise people and objects. When they throw their power around you, you are in a force-field of such love that nothing can harm you. Archangel Michael commands the Angels of Protection.

> During a phone-in a listener told us that she was crossing a road in her invalid carriage. Suddenly a youngster in a sports car raced round the corner and hit her. As she flew up into the air she thought she was finished but she floated down to Earth in slow motion. She had one tiny bruise. None of the horrified onlookers could believe what they had seen but she felt her angel holding her.

I remember the audible gasp that went round the auditorium when a lady told us her extraordinary story.

> When she was ten years old she used to swim regularly, training in her parents' swimming pool. One night she was ready for her training session. She dived into the water and as she hit it, something lifted her back up and on to the side again. She was back at the place where she started but her face was wet, so she knew that she had not imagined it.

At that moment all the lights in the house went on!

She threw on her wrap and ran inside. She said to her brother, who was in the house, 'Why have you put all the lights on?' He said that he had not. He had been sitting there all the time. Totally shocked, she went to bed.

In the morning she told her parents about the weird happening and her father went down with her to the swimming pool. They found that the electric cable had snapped and was lying in the water.

So the angels saved her life. Clearly it was not her time to die.

When an angel saves your life it is often a wake-up call which jolts you into life change.

Peter Feldman was saved not once but twice within a week by the angels. His soul was determined he take notice and indeed he did.

One day he was driving too fast down a hill and there was a traffic jam in front of him. As he braked, the car skidded into the path of a stream of traffic coming towards him. He just knew he would be killed. But a gap opened up like magic for him and he skidded straight through the gap and came to rest on the kerb. He was considerably shaken by this miracle.

Five days later he was getting out of his car in his driveway when a man appeared beside him and put a gun to his head. Peter said, 'Take the car but don't shoot.' But the man just stood there, menacing him until he panicked and shouted. Then the man shot him in the stomach. He jumped into the car and raced off, leaving Peter in a pool of blood.

His wife heard his scream and called the police. Eventually they got him inside the house, clearly badly injured, as they waited for an ambulance.

Suddenly he felt enveloped in warmth and love and an angel of light held him. He said to her, 'Am I going to die?'

She said, 'No. You will be alright. You have got too much to do.'

The bullet had missed all the vital organs and he was OK. He was ready to change his life and he did. He is one of the most genuine and gifted journalists I know *and* he has the courage to talk and write about angels.

A lady told me that her husband was working in Germany, where he often did business. He stayed the night in a hotel and in the morning he got into the car and drove away. To his horror he found himself driving the wrong way down the slip road on to the autobahn towards the oncoming cars. Instantly he called to the angels for help.

He did not know what happened but the very next instant he was on the other carriageway in the outside lane driving in the stream of traffic.

The angels are working overtime to protect you.

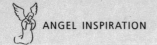

Service work

Sit quietly and direct angels to help those in need. You can either make this specific to a place or person or send out a general prayer for the angels to help those who need to be protected.

CHAPTER TWENTY

Michael Cuts the Cords

You can have anything, but the moment you are attached to it, you are bound. You can have a beautiful house to live in but if you need it for your sense of security, a psychic cord binds you to it and you are tied. You can have a powerful job and riches and be a Master. However, if you need your job or riches for your sense of self-worth, you become a slave. You can have a deeply loving relationship but if it becomes co-dependent, subtle psychic cords bind you to your partner and you are no longer free. All these things become balls and chains holding you down to the lower dimensions.

You can also be attached to old painful memories, hurts, angers, jealousy and a hundred negative feelings or beliefs, which bind you to a lower way of being. They tie you up in dependence, unhappiness, poverty and ill-health.

A Master has his or her heart's desire while remaining unattached and free.

You can ask Archangel Michael to use his mighty sword to cut the cords which tie you to the past and give you the courage and strength to move into the new and better.

When Archangel Michael uses his sword to cut the cords which bind people and situations, it has a dramatic influence on every area of their life including their health.

Jackie Roxborough told me this story of courage, endurance and a miracle.

In February 1994 Jackie was diagnosed with diabetes mellitus and became severely ill. Underlying all was a thyroid condition. As she had a very strong belief that we have the ability to turn around such problems, she set about exploring complementary methods of healing, both physically and metaphysically.

For almost two years she worked to regain her health without the use of insulin, despite the unsympathetic attitude of orthodox doctors. During this time she became very emaciated, eventually becoming insulin-dependent. By then her body had become insulin-resistant, so that she experienced a further two years of 'lost' time, feeling distant and often sleeping for days and weeks at a time.

In this critical state she met a private doctor who runs the National Thyroid Clinic and within four days the fuzzy world lifted and she began to recover.

Then once again she became desperately ill. This time her doctor was convinced she had a very severe condition known as temporal arteritis and she was advised that she could drop dead at any moment without steroids. Jackie was reluctant to take medication. The doctor was fantastic and checked out her presenting condition with registrars and top people in the field. All confirmed the diagnosis. Her life was in extreme danger.

Each day she had a blood test and her doctor would ring her to tell her that the news was very bad. As the week progressed Jackie was becoming more and more panic-stricken, so she made a deal with her doctor to take the medication and have a biopsy if the last blood test came back the same or worse.

That day she made a connection with a healer, who told her to ask for help from Archangel Michael. She was to call on him to cut the ties that bind with his sword, so that she could face the situation honestly. She did this and it was a very powerful moment in her life. Archangel Michael cut the ties from all her earthly connections and she felt totally at peace.

The following day she had another blood test. Again it was severely abnormal.

That night she meditated to ask for more help to prepare for what seemed the inevitable. Then at the end of her bed there appeared the most stunningly beautiful golden angelic being, about ten feet tall. The radiating gold light was breathtaking and of pure love. She felt even greater peace than the day before.

The following day the doctor rang to say that the blood test was completely normal.

This beautiful and brave woman wrote to me: 'Although I was taken to the absolute edge of trust and belief, I still look on all of my journey for health as the most positive enlightening experience I could have had. My health is much better and stronger now. Spiritually I am developing more awareness and furthermore, I have a better understanding of my role in life, which becomes more clarified day by day. I am to work with sound to help raise the vibration of humanity. I feel very humbled by being given such a task.'

I used to help people cut the cords by asking them to visualise themselves in one section of a figure of eight, and the thing or person they were releasing in the other. It is indeed most effective. However, since I worked with the angels and have experienced the power of Archangel Michael to sever binding cords, I always call on him to cut them. His light can transmute the negative energy to the core of the problem.

You cannot cut the cords between other people without their permission, for that would contravene their free will.

However, you can call on Archangel Michael to cut the collective cords that bind humanity. Your prayer will add to the thread of other prayers going to him and will enable him to take action.

Frequently a country holds on to anger about a long-past war or injustice. This keeps it stuck. Groups of people cling on to fear of certain diseases. Many are psychically attached to the great thought form about AIDS. As their panic tugs this thought form towards them, they open themselves up to it.

In some countries many citizens are attached to a collective belief that they must have material wealth in order to be worthwhile. In others the collective belief is that there is no way out of poverty.

Some religions hold on to a belief in persecution, thus pulling it towards them.

It is time now for awakened humanity to invoke Archangel Michael to cut these thought-forms away and transmute them.

Service work

On a regular basis ask Archangel Michael to cut the psychic cords which attach you to situations, objects, negative emotions and people (except your young children).

Pray to Archangel Michael to cut the collective ties of groups of people to negative beliefs and emotions about past events or fears and transmute them.

CHAPTER TWENTY-ONE

Archangel Jophiel

The mighty Archangel Jophiel is the Angel of Wisdom and Illumination. He and his Archeia or twin flame, Christine, bring down the wisdom from the Godhead. As Christine's name suggests, she is one with the consciousness of Christ. Their mission is to illuminate humankind with true understandings of the teachings of the Radiant Ones and light the highest pathway for each individual. They help draw down your perfect blueprint. They release great currents of light which flow round the brain and remove negativity.

Archangel Jophiel helps to focus you away from the personality and the material to the Christ mind. He brings enlightenment and understanding, health and wealth. With wisdom and clarity comes absence of fear.

Jophiel and Christine are Archangels of the second ray, the yellow ray. Yellow is the mental colour, which deepens to gold as you open to more wisdom. They are particularly involved with helping teachers and students at schools, colleges and universities and will enable you to absorb and retain information, study and pass examinations.

They also help people to be faithful to a belief or vision or to stand by an important cause.

Archangel Jophiel works closely with Lord Kuthumi, who is the Master or Chohan of the deep blue aspect of the second ray. This is known as the love-wisdom ray.

Lord Kuthumi is a member of the Brotherhood of Golden Robe, those who take on the pain of world. He has an etheric retreat at Machu Pichu. In past incarnations he was Pythagoras, bringing in sacred geometry and the music of the spheres. He was the wise man, Balthazar, Shah Jahan, who had the Taj Mahal built, and St Francis.

Invoke the Higher Beings of this ray if you wish to be able to impart truth and understanding to others, or if you desire more tact and foresight, wisdom, intuition and the ability to learn about your subject.

Archangel Jophiel is in charge of expanding the crown chakra in all of humanity to enable all to connect with their Higher Selves. The crown chakra is the thousand-petal lotus at the top of the head. As each petal of the flower opens we are able to receive more divine illumination. The golden crown, which is worn by royalty and those who attain high office, represents the opening of this chakra to connect with God.

The day on which Archangel Jophiel's influence is strongest on the planet is Sunday and his etheric retreat is south of the Great Wall of China. Command your spirit to go there in meditation, or at night if you wish to receive illumination or wisdom or to merge with your Higher Self or be helped with your studies or teachings.

Whenever you are stuck in a problem and suddenly the solution is obvious, one of Archangel Jophiel's angels has probably illumined your mind. Flashes of inspiration come from him too.

If you are giving a talk, call on Archangel Jophiel to help you. Should you dry up or need more flow or inspiration, send out a thought and he will be there.

Rosemary said that she often worked with her angel, who was a huge silver being. One day she was giving a presentation and someone asked a question. To her embarrassment she simply froze. Nothing came through and she could not answer the question.

Then she quietly asked her angel to speak through her and suddenly the answer came flooding into her mind and she was able to reply easily.

Afterwards a lady from the audience came up to her and said. 'A beautiful silver angel talked to you in the middle of your talk.'

At a workshop I discussed the many ways in which Archangel Jophiel can help teachers. A few days later I received this letter from a teacher who attended with her friend.

'The friend who accompanied me to your workshop teaches a class of thirty-six ten-year-old boys. On Monday I went into her class and the peace was so profound I called one of the male teachers in and asked him to spend half a minute there without any explanation to him. He came out and asked, "What happened? Can I buy into this?"'

Whenever you think of a school, college or university, or pass one in your car, ask Archangel Jophiel and his angels to illumine the minds of teachers and students alike. Of course you can ask for help for individual children.

You may not realise what an impact you can have. Every single time you ask the angels to help a situation, one or more are delegated to do the work. It is only because they are working on a frequency beyond our range that we do not normally see what happens.

> Debbie Mann has frequently seen angels. She communicates with them all the time. She told me that on one occasion she asked the angels to give healing to the children in school. She was standing at the school gates waiting for her daughter as she made this request.
>
> Immediately a huge angel appeared like a great light, which was totally magnificent, and swept the area with love and healing energy. Imagine the difference it made.

The Angels of Illumination and Wisdom will also help ambassadors, politicians and people who are in a position of power and influence, so ask these wonderful beings to guide and help them too for the highest good of all.

Service work

Focus on an educational establishment and ask Archangel Jophiel and the Angels of Illumination and Wisdom to help all the students and teachers there. Visualize the golden colour filling the building and touching everyone in it.

You can also direct these angels into town halls, parliament buildings, courts of justice and any place where important decisions are taken.

CHAPTER TWENTY-TWO

Archangel Chamuel

The mighty Archangel Chamuel is the Angel of Love, who helps you to open your heart by expanding the flame of love within you. He pours unconditional love into you and enables you to express love through creativity of all sorts.

His twin flame is Charity, who touches you with the feminine qualities of tenderness, mercy, compassion and empathy. Together they focus on expanding the heart energy of peacemakers, philosophers and those who wish to spread the higher truths. They pour love and light into the hearts of artists, writers, sculptors and all who are working from their hearts. They impress all kinds of creators to enable them to express the Christ Consciousness in their work.

Archangel Chamuel and Charity are bringing in the third ray, which is the pink ray of creative, active intelligence. It is the ray of unconditional love. Those who express the highest of this ray are dedicated, sincere, highly imaginative, clear-minded and organised. Those on this ray who are less evolved may need to work on obstinacy, absentmindedness, commonsense and tolerance. The Archangels will help them.

They work closely with Serapis Bey, the Chohan or Master of the third ray, who came originally from Venus to assist our planet. He is the only Ascended Master who works with the Seraphim, those ineffable beings who surround the Godhead and maintain the vibration of the Creation. Serapis Bey was, in previous lives, a priest in Atlantis; also Akhenaton IV and Amenophis, two of the great Pharoahs. His ascension seat is in Luxor. If you feel you have an Egyptian connection, visit his ascension seat in meditation or sleep and you may open up to your former gifts and wisdom.

Naturally Archangel Chamuel is in charge of the development of the heart chakra in all people. At the third-dimensional level this is green, the colour of nature, with a pink centre. As you evolve it becomes lighter pink and the spiritual colour violet develops. The fourth-dimensional heart chakra is pale pink violet. At the fifth dimension, when you become an Ascended Master, it is pure white. Serapis Bey is Keeper of the White Flame for humanity. When you expand your heart chakra to this level, you carry the Christ Consciousness. Your cosmic heart is now open and you connect to the love of the cosmos.

Call on Chamuel and Charity if your heart is broken or bruised. They will help you to mend it. If it is blocked through pain or inability to forgive another, ask them to help you find forgiveness. They will melt the stones within you caused by unresolved anger, hurt, fear and guilt.

Chamuel's spiritual retreat is at St Louis, Missouri, and it is a real heart-awakener to ask to go there in your dream state at night. You will be bathed in the love of the Archangel during your sleep.

The day in which his energy is most powerfully reflected to Earth is Monday.

Archangel Chamuel is in charge of all the Angels of Love. They will come to you in pure compassion and love when you need them. Angels of Love are those who help you to find lost objects. Just ask quietly for their help and they will return your possessions if it is possible.

I receive many letters from people who have asked the Angels of Love to help them, like this one from Lucy. Every day she asked the angels to look after her and she really expected them to do so. One night she lost her purse at a night-club. The following day, when she returned to see if it had been found, she spoke to several people without success. Then she asked the cloakroom attendant, who had found it, with all the money still intact.

Angels of Love will do whatever they can within the guidelines of Spiritual Law to smooth your life.

Here is a beautiful thing to do, which will make you feel much happier. Close your eyes and ask the angels to pour an angelic love shower over you. If you are sensitive, you will feel it softly pouring down over you.

Service work

Close your eyes and ask the Angels of Love to pour a love shower over a person or place in need.

CHAPTER TWENTY-THREE

Chamuel's Angels of Love

The angels cannot prevent you from experiencing loss and bereavement if that is part of the divine plan to which your soul has agreed. However, they can comfort you.

Marie Pead's son Martin was killed on the North West Hutton Oil Rig, north of the Shetland Islands. It was several days after the tragedy before the family could go to the funeral parlour to be with him.

Marie was completely overwhelmed with grief and asked to be alone with the coffin. She felt so desperate that she lay on the coffin to be closer to her son. As she did so, she felt the presence of angels and the angels were weeping with her.

Three years after her son died, she was still feeling very sad. One day she was sitting quietly at home when an angel came into the room. He stood in a radiant light and said to her, 'We here from our realm have come to let you experience for a brief moment the love from this realm.' The angel filled her with love past all understanding. Marie said, 'I have never forgotten it.'

The death of a loved one often leaves us humans feeling totally bereft and lost.

Carol told us how devastated she felt when her friend died. She was inconsolable. As she sat at home crying, suddenly she was filled with love inside. She was filled with love for everyone. She felt the glorious light growing inside her and radiating around her. She was luminous.

When her husband came home she ran to the door and flung her arms around him, saying, 'I love you and I love everyone and everything.'

Then gradually the light and incredible feeling faded.

Angels of Love appear unexpectedly in response to people who are working with their hearts open.

Joy works with disabled people. One day, she was giving healing to a girl called Sarah, whose parents were in the room with them.

Suddenly, in the middle of the healing a huge angel enfolded Joy, Sarah and her parents. All four of them were held in his great light. Time stopped. Then the angel withdrew and they looked at each other in silent amazement. They were all completely filled with love.

Angels of Love will do whatever they can to heal a hurting heart.

Carolyn told me that many years ago her thirteen-year-old brother Paul was killed in a car accident. Her father was absolutely devastated.

A few months after his death Carolyn dreamt that she was with her father when a golden figure entered the room and held his hand out to him and said, 'Come with me.' Her father took his hand and went with him.

The dream was so vivid that she woke thinking that her father had died. She looked at her watch and saw that it was two-fifteen in the morning. She wanted to get up to see if he was alright but she could not get out of bed. It was as if a force had been put round her to keep her there. At last she decided to go back to sleep again.

The following morning her father came to her room and said, 'Paul came to me in the night.' She asked what time it was and he said, 'It was two-fifteen this morning.'

She knew then that the angels had brought Paul to comfort her father and held her in bed so that she did not disturb his visit.

Angels will do what they can to look after children. If the child's higher self, or soul, has agreed to those conditions before they were born, they are obliged to stand by and watch without interfering.

Sometimes prayers from relatives or mass prayers from sincere people open up a pathway which allows them to help.

A woman told this heart-rending story of her early childhood in wartime Germany. She was three and a

half when her parents were sent to a concentration camp. She was all on her own.

A horrible couple fostered her. They used to lock her in a cupboard at night and she was not allowed to speak or use the toilet. One night she desperately wanted to go to the toilet but was too frightened to knock and ask to be let out.

Suddenly a light appeared to her and in that light was an angel, which enfolded her with love. She said, 'I have never known fear since that moment.'

Angels of Love look after lost items and help return them to you.

My friend Elizabeth told me that she always asked the Angels of Lost Items for help. A few days earlier she had a call from a friend who was in a real state. She was due to be teaching in a nearby town and had put all her notes and books in the car and she had lost the key! She wanted Elizabeth to take her to the college as quickly as possible, even without her notes.

As she drove to her friend's house, Elizabeth invoked the Angels of Lost Items and asked them to find the key. When she turned into the drive, her friend was holding the car key, which she had found thirty seconds before.

The Angels of Love will also look after things until you can fetch them.

My friend Soozie Holbeche was travelling in Egypt with her husband. They took a train, then a taxi to a hotel. When they arrived her husband was very upset to discover he had lost his favourite fountain pen. He must have left it on the train and was sure it would have disappeared by now.

Soozie immediately put a ring of gold around the pen, wherever it was, and asked the angels to look after it. Her husband took the taxi straight back to the station and there was the pen lying under the seat in the carriage, where he had dropped it.

Never despair if you lose something. Relax and ask the angels to keep it safe for you and help you find it. If it is yours by divine right, they will look after it. If it is not, just let it go.

Service work

If you see or read in the media that someone has a hurting heart, sit quietly and direct Archangel Chamuel's Angels of Love to pour love into their heart and enfold them in their wings.

CHAPTER TWENTY-FOUR

Archangel Gabriel

The mighty Archangel Gabriel is the Angel of Harmony, Beauty, Purification and Art.

His twin flame is Hope, the pure flame of the divine mother. She is the divine spark that resides in the heart chakra, who gives you hope and strength to move on instead of staying stuck.

Gabriel offers hope, spirituality and love and helps your intuition. He stands for clarity, purity, order and discipline. If you need more of these qualities, call on him.

Gabriel is in charge of the Angels of Guidance and their task is to help you understand the life plan you agreed with your spiritual advisers and the Lords of Karma before you embarked on your life.

Gabriel and Hope remind you of the perfect vision of yourself, your divine potential. They will guide you about the next step in your life or, if you are ready, reveal your mission on Earth to you. You can in meditation ask Archangel Gabriel to light up within your aura the symbols of your life work so that you attract the perfect people and opportunities. He will give you guidance to help you on your path. So watch for the signals. He will also give you the discipline, staying power, efficiency and clarity to stay on your pathway.

If you wake up in the morning with inspiration about

your next step, with new ideas about your job or what to do next, you have probably visited his spiritual retreat during sleep.

When there seems to be opposition to your mission, Gabriel's Angels of Guidance will help to clear the opposition, if you ask them to.

He works in the pure white light, the purest essence of every ray. If you need purification you can ask to go to his spiritual retreat at Mount Shasta during sleep or meditation and he will work on your energy to release old memories, patterns or beliefs that are keeping you stuck. Many seekers on the ascension pathway try to raise their light levels, when in fact they need to clear out the old before they can take in more light. Gabriel will work with you in this.

He also has a spiritual retreat at Findhorn for purification and helping souls to awaken.

Every human being goes through a journey to the light. When you decide to leave the consciousness of the lower, material world you undergo a crucifixion, which is an extremely painful testing time. You may be crucified by pain or by the loss of loved ones, job or reputation. You then move to a higher level of awareness. After crucifixion comes resurrection, when you can step on to your ascension pathway. This will be punctuated by initiations, which are even more painful than a crucifixion, as all that you hold important is stripped away. This is to test your attachment to ego.

No two people have the same journey. If you have passed these tests in another life, your soul may decide not to call on you to go through them again.

Gabriel assists in your resurrection, in the ritual of

ascension, and attends your ascension ceremony on the inner planes.

Archangel Gabriel works on the fourth ray, and his co-worker, the Ascended Master of Shambhalla in charge of the emerald-green aspect of the fourth ray, is Paul the Venetian. His task is to bring art and music more deeply into the experiential realms, so that people can truly feel what an artist or musician is expressing. He and Archangel Gabriel naturally work closely together to bring forward the new cosmic concepts for the arts, one from a human perspective, the other from an angelic one.

When you express your lower will, conflict and struggle ensue. The higher expression results in total harmony.

Fourth-ray people are architects, builders, musicians, artists, spiritual leaders and spiritual scientists of all kinds. Archangel Gabriel is overlighting them.

The day his energy is felt most strongly on the planet is Friday, which is a good day to invoke him and connect to his energy.

The chakra which Gabriel is helping to develop on Earth is the base chakra. At the physical, third-dimensional level, this is red and concerned with your survival on this planet. As your chakra develops into a fourth-dimensional one it becomes a luminous pearl white, enabling you to live your life in joy, and lighting up all the cells of your body. Your fifth-dimensional base chakra is platinum. When your fifth-dimensional chakra is anchored and integrated, you live as a Master, in bliss. You are then fully on your ascension pathway and Archangel Gabriel is overseeing it.

Originally the base centre and the sacral centre in the abdomen, which is the emotional and sexual centre, were one. Now they have been differentiated and Archangel Gabriel oversees the development and evolution of both of them.

Gabriel is the Angel of Childbirth and is always in attendance as a new soul comes into Earth. Ask for his blessing on all newborn creatures. I was talking to an extremely sensible and grounded nurse, who told me that many of her colleagues had seen angels present at the birth of babies. It was Gabriel who told Mary that she was to be the mother of the Son of God.

It was Archangel Gabriel who inspired Mohammed to found Islam.

Service work

Quietly direct Archangel Gabriel's Angels of Purity and Guidance to radiate their white light to people on Earth who are confused or depressed.

When you sense that someone is lost or directionless, ask Archangel Gabriel to guide them on to their path.

CHAPTER TWENTY-FIVE

Archangel Raphael

The mighty Archangel Raphael is the Angel of Healing, Abundance, Creativity, Truth and Vision. His twin flame is Mary, mother of Jesus, known as Queen of the Angels.

Raphael carries the masculine, doing, creating, active energy of healing, while Mary holds the feminine energy of nurturing, compassion, grace and mercy. She is mothering and protective. Their presence is always available to assist doctors, nurses, healers and mothers.

Raphael is in charge of the development of the third-eye chakra in humanity. The qualities of this chakra are vision, intuition, concentration, focus and truth. Raphael helps you to develop inner vision, to be a seer. He is patron saint of the blind.

The third eye works on many levels. Clairvoyance or clear sight is the ability to see beyond the physical into the inner realms. When the third eye is forced open through trauma, shock, starvation, alcohol or drugs, you may find yourself seeing into the lower astral dimensions. This is the frequency band in which negative entities, demons, nasty thought-forms and emotions reside. It can be very frightening and disturbing. Mental hospitals are full of people who have opened up their third eye at this level. When this happens, it is a warning to close your chakra down, then raise your consciousness and call on Archangel Raphael for help and healing.

Even if your third eye opens too quickly and you 'flip out' into the higher realms, it is vital to ground yourself and call on Archangel Raphael for help.

Many clairvoyants are extremely spiritual souls, who have earned their gifts over lifetimes of service. However, the fact that someone is psychic does not necessarily make them spiritual. To be clairvoyant without being spiritual is a two-edged sword. It offers power without wisdom.

A number of people seek to develop clairvoyance and feel that it is a sign that they are progressing. Indeed, it means that another petal of your third eye is opening, but how you use the information is more important for your growth than what you can see. Call on Archangel Raphael to help you develop in a perfect way.

On a truly spiritual path your intuition is honed. This is the ability to listen to your inner wisdom, which is connected to universal wisdom. Intuition requires a much higher frequency than clairvoyance and an intuitive has to lower the vibration of his or her third eye in order to see. An intuitive *knows*, without necessarily seeing.

The ultimate aim of developing the third-eye chakra is to connect to the eye of Horus, the spiritual eye, which is shrouded from most people by the seven veils of illusion. This is the journey of connection to the divine. Then you become a true seer or visionary. At this stage you become aware of the presence of angels, higher guides and Masters. You may not see them but you will know they are there.

I had periods of being quite clairvoyant. It seemed glorious and exciting, though when I first opened up I was still full of fear, rage, guilt and the emotions that connected me to the lower astral planes. I saw some scary things as well as beautiful ones. As I worked to purify myself, that stopped and I opened up to the higher realms of angels. Now I rarely 'see'. I assume that if it is important for me to see something I will be shown it. However, I *know*.

I love it when I am with clairvoyants because they see what I know. On one occasion I was in full flow during a live radio broadcast, when the interviewer suddenly interrupted to ask me what his angel was like! I was just about to say that I couldn't see it, when I had a total knowing that it was a beautiful pure white angel standing by his right shoulder, literally pouring illumination on to him. The angel was helping him greatly with his work. He was thrilled to hear this.

Anne Hogan, a lifelong natural clairvoyant and healer, was with me. She told him afterwards that she too could see his pure white angel standing at his right-hand side, helping him. She emphasized just how much love and beauty the angel was radiating through him.

Archangel Raphael is the Angel of Abundance. The third eye governs the twin functions of focus and vision. Focus or concentration is left brain, whereas creative visualisation is right brain. When you can totally concentrate on your heart's desire and visualise it clearly, you are able to manifest it. Raphael assists you to concentrate and focus. He enhances your ability to create through visualisation. When you call on his help, you co-create abundance in a perfect way.

He works on the fifth ray, in close cooperation with

Master Hilarian, on the orange vibration. This is the ray of science, knowledge and research. On one level it is a mind ray, but because it accesses the higher mental body, which is the realm of the soul, it carries the quality of unconditional love. Together, these Great Ones help you to find truth.

Archangel Raphael works on the emerald-green ray of the heart. His healing power is directed to the dissolution of negative blocks, which cause dis-ease, and to the positive power of love, which manifests as health.

Helena Dodds, who promoted some of my seminars in South Africa and became a good friend, listened to my angel tape before I met her. During the Archangel meditation she directed herself to Archangel Raphael's retreat because for some time she had had a bad cough. Her chest hurt and her throat felt as if needles were being stuck in it. She wanted angel healing.

She e-mailed me afterwards that she had an experience beyond anything she had ever known before. As she listened to the tape, tremendous heat flowed into her hands. She placed them on her chest and throat. The cough went immediately. She said that the energy was quite amazing and she was blown away by it.

Later in the day, her cousin came to visit her and they sat together on the terrace to chat. Helena told her cousin about her experience. As she did so she looked down at the bricks of her patio and there nestled a little white feather. She swore that the only birds in the area were black drongos.

Do direct your spirit to visit Archangel Raphael's spiritual retreat, which is in the etheric above Fatima, Portugal, at night, or in meditation, if you wish to receive his wonderful light.

Here is a story about Archangel Raphael's response to the power of a mother's prayer, given to me by Wendy Goodchild, who is a natural psychic and healer. Ever since he was three years old, her son Zach has had gluten intolerance. Every now and again a blockage will build up in his intestines, causing fatigue, pain, high temperature and infection. He invariably ended up in intensive care, very ill.

A few years ago, Wendy decided she would no longer hand him over to the medical system. She would trust her dowsing, complementary therapy and prayer. She wrote, 'It took a huge leap of faith when he had all the symptoms as before, not to call the emergency services.

'Zach was lying on my bed, ill again, with another blockage, and my mother's antennae were telling me it was all taking hold again. The prickly feeling of alarm was building up. I gave him some healing but it wasn't enough. I held his hands and asked him to ask for Raphael to come and help us. Zach fell asleep and I carried on praying.

'All of a sudden I was aware of the room becoming very hot and a very bold, vibrant green. The stillness of my mind was wonderful.

'One of my other sons entered the room and said, "Phew, it's too hot in here," And he left.

'The green ebbed away and I stroked the air around Zach gently. Twenty minutes later I was standing watching the same child outside playing in the garden.'
He has never returned to that critical state.

Archangel Raphael's day is Wednesday, so if you meditate or invoke him on that day it will be more powerful and effective.

Service work
When people are 'blind' to the spiritual truths, ask Archangel Raphael to open their eyes to higher possibilities and the true glory of the Universe.

CHAPTER TWENTY-SIX

Mary, Queen of the Angels

Mary has embodied the divine feminine in several life-times. In Atlantis she was adept in the use of crystals for healing. She was the Moon Goddess Ishtar in Mesopotamia. She was the Goddess Isis in Egypt where she helped initiates in the temples. In Greece she was Diana, Goddess of the Moon and Nature. Her best-known and most revered life was as the mother of Jesus Christ.

She is the twin flame of Archangel Raphael and is known as Queen of the Angels, radiating compassion and love. Her task is to bring healing and love to all, especially babies and children.

Her colour is the light blue of healing and she appears to many people to give them faith and hope.

A few years ago Mother Mary came to me when I was giving healing to my daughter Lauren, who was very ill as a baby. She told me that a mother normally has blue in her aura, which enfolds the baby, healing, nurturing and protecting it. Because Lauren was in hospital for so long, she did not receive this blue light. Mary said she had come to put the missing energy into Lauren's aura so that she could at last heal the trauma of her child-hood illness and separation.

Since then Mary has frequently appeared at workshops

with her wonderful magnetic energy to heal people's babyhood and childhood. She glides among the participants touching them as necessary and pouring her beautiful blue light into their auras.

More and more healers and therapists are telling me that Mary is working with them with their clients.

It is quite magical to imagine you are holding your own inner child or baby with Mother Mary's blue cloak around both of you. Whether you are aware of it or not, you have automatically called her presence to you and healing is taking place.

You have only to think of Mary and she is by your side, touching you with love, healing and compassion. For centuries she has been offering to help but we have not been ready. Your task is to be open and receptive to the possibilities she brings now.

When you pray for help for yourself or another, miracles sometimes take place. Here is an example.

Barbara was at a nursing home to have a small operation. The surgeon started his operating list at 2.30 p.m.

Suddenly there was frantic activity. A two-year-old was having her tonsils out. The surgeon had severed her cirrhotic artery. There was blood everywhere and there was no more blood in the blood bank.

The mother was absolutely frantic. The grandfather was sitting hitting his head on the wall. *So Barbara sat quietly waiting and prayed for the child.* Just as hope was fading, she saw Mother Mary come to the child.

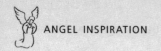

> Absolute silence fell and at that moment the child's heart stopped pumping blood out.
>
> They knew she would be alright. She was.

Never underestimate the power of prayer. Quality calm and pure prayer, with compassion calls on the Queen of the Angels, meaning she can create miracles.

Mary comes with the greatest compassion to youngsters, especially those who feel lost. Many of the teenagers who take drugs and alcohol to bury their pain are really seeking spirit. Their antisocial behaviour disguises a desperate longing for an elusive higher way of living.

> Wendy Goodchild is a healer who works on the ray of compassion. When her fifteen-year-old son John caught a virus he was taken into hospital for blood tests and put into an adult ward. The youth in the next bed had been admitted as a result of drug abuse. Aged about nineteen, he was loud, disruptive and rude to the nurses. Emotionally he was hurting badly, for his mother was a depressive and his father could not cope with him and did not want him.
>
> Wendy gave her son healing and then took out her pendulum to dowse for some information. The lad in the next bed was intrigued. He asked for an explanation and was very interested. She explained what she was doing and he asked lots of questions and wanted to try dowsing. She offered him a grounding meditation and some healing before he had a go.

He eyed them up from a distance, then returned to say, 'Yes, please.' After a short meditation his eyes opened wide and he said he had heard the name 'Michael'. Wendy was able to tell him it was the Archangel Michael and he was being blessed as the moment was right to let go of unwanted ties in his life. He had learnt and must moved on. So they asked for the ties to be cut.

When that was done, again his eyes shot open and he said he had heard the word 'Mary'. Wendy said that this was Mother Mary coming to give healing and love to his inner child. They relaxed with the energy for some time and when he opened his eyes, they looked vibrant and clear.

They joked that the feeling was a lot cheaper than the drugs he had been using.

The following day a nurse came over and said, 'I don't know what you did with him yesterday, but thank you. He is so much calmer.'

Service work

When you sense that someone's inner child is hurting, ask Mother Mary to enfold them in her blue cloak and comfort them.

Visualise her blue cloak being placed around newborn babies.

CHAPTER TWENTY-SEVEN

Raphael's Angels of Healing

Angels are God's healers. They are beings of love, compassion, mercy and grace. Because angels carry such a high-frequency current their presence can affect you deeply.

They heal in three ways. Sometimes when they touch you they activate your own self-healing mechanism. At other times they dissolve the emotional and mental blocks that underlie your disease, so that it automatically heals.

Occasionally they intercede on the ray of mercy and a miraculous healing occurs. However, they will only perform a miracle if this is in your highest interest. If your soul needs a lesson, which is manifesting as an illness, it would not be appropriate to take that learning experience away from you.

Susan Seddon was shocked when she was diagnosed with breast cancer. On the night before she was due to go into hospital for surgery, she got into bed and lay on her tummy feeling very alone. She just needed a hug.

Out of the corner of her eye, she saw mist and thought it was a fire. Very slowly she turned over on to her back, trying to smell smoke.

To her amazement the whole room was lit up. It was full of tiny white feathery angels, each in a ball of light, who filled her with love, lightness and bliss. All her fear went and never returned.

She is now totally healed and as a result of her experience with the angels she has created a sanctuary to heal and comfort others. She is able to take their fear away just as the angels did for her.

When angels help you in any way, you then contain that light which you can use to help, comfort and heal others.

The Angels of Healing have enormous compassion. They do hear your prayers and if it is possible under Spiritual Law to help, they will do so.

Jesse's friend had a riding accident and as a result was badly brain-damaged. Jesse was devastated and drove to the hospital to see him several times a week. He was like a different person and the doctors told her that he would never improve. One day she left the hospital and sat in the car. 'Please let him be okay,' she implored from the bottom of her heart.

Suddenly an angel appeared and smiled at her. From that moment she knew that he would be alright but she couldn't tell anyone. She absolutely knew he would get better, and against all the odds he made a total recovery.

Never give up hope. Continue to hold the vision of perfect health for everyone. That is also God's vision for them and faith activates miracles.

Angels of Healing do not just heal. As the following story demonstrates, they hold you totally steady if that is what is needed. They will do anything that is necessary for you.

A woman told us how her son had dived into a rock pool and hit his head. He had fractured three vertebrae at the top of his neck and she and her daughter sat by him in the hospital, absolutely fearing the worst. Then a huge golden angel came in and sat by his head. Both of them saw it. They were convinced he would be alright.

As a result of the three fractured unstable vertebrae he was in traction for twelve weeks. They were told that the top one was broken and if he had moved very slightly he would have died. With the other fracture, if he had moved he would have become a quadriplegic. But he was perfectly, 100 per cent, OK. They saw the golden angel sitting by him twice more.

If you are invoking the Angels of Healing, always tell them what you really want. The importance of this was demonstrated to me a few years ago when I was facilitating a residential workshop. One of the participants had an abscess on her tooth. She had suffered several in the past and invariably had to take antibiotics. In the night it became very painful and she could not sleep. Eventually she asked the angels to take the pain away and within a short time it dissolved. She slept. The following day her face was still very swollen though the pain had gone. Gradually, over the course of the next few days, the swelling went down and she did not have to take antibiotics. We all joked that next time she must ask for the swelling to be taken away too.

A few months later I was facilitating another residential workshop and again a participant had an abscess on her tooth. Her face was swollen and she was in considerable pain. I told her the previous story and, when she went to bed she asked the angels to take the pain, the infection and the swelling away. When she woke in the morning it had gone completely.

The Angels of Mercy are the highest-ranking angels. They do respond to your call for help as Ginny Burman and Nick Morris were privileged to discover.

> Ginny had been working as a spiritual healer for fifteen years. One Saturday morning a young man came to her Healing Centre, looking so ill and forlorn that it touched her heart. After several visits he was still suffering from ME and was completely debilitated. His heart centre had closed and he was unable to work as a painter. One Saturday he was in deep despair, his eyes were dull, his skin cold and white. He was thin and drawn.
>
> As Ginny tuned in for the healing energy, her heart chakra opened wide, so that all of Nick's anguish flooded in. She felt his pain and silently cried out, 'For the love of God let the Angel of Mercy come down and help this boy.'

This is what she wrote: 'At that moment before me and in front of Nick appeared a magnificent creature, shimmering in pure white and silver. The Angel was well over six feet tall and the light shone for a huge distance all around the being. The angel was so beautiful, dressed in a robe and with wings, not at all how I would have perceived an angel to be.

'I was filled with awesome love, which filled every minute particle of me. I thought I was going to explode with love, it was so overpowering. I was told that Nick could call on the angel any time he felt the need.'

The experience left Ginny overcome with love and awe.

While they both expected immediate results, Nick's healing has been gradual but he is now painting again and he has just exhibited. More exhibitions are booked. His eyes are bright. His skin is a healthy colour and he is much happier.

Ginny added, 'I know his angel has made it all happen and I feel very privileged to have seen the angel. It is an experience I will never forget but cannot do justice to in words.'

Angels are always delighted to work through you. If you wish to channel their healing energy for someone else, ask for it and trust that it will come through you.

Patricia was awaiting a replacement operation when she attended a Healing with Angels workshop. When I told the group that we were going to work in pairs to bring angelic healing through for a partner, she thought, 'No chance. I can't even stand, my arthritis is so bad.' However, after she received healing from the angels through her partner, she found she could stand easily and without pain.

That night she went to bed looking forward to the second day of the course. In the middle of the night she woke and could not get back to sleep. At last she called to the angels, 'Please, please help me to sleep, so that I'm ready for tomorrow.'

Patricia fell asleep immediately and woke with a little white feather on her thigh. For the first time in months she had no pain. She still had to have her operation but she knew all would go well. The angels had blessed her.

When you need healing of any description, ask the angels. They will help you in some way.

Service work

Set aside a beautiful bowl and place it in a special place with a candle. Light the candle and write down the names of people who want healing. It does not matter whether you know them or not. As you write the names and place them in the bowl, picture the person in perfect health and ask the angels to help them for their highest good. Know that angels will never contravene free will.

A week later, take out the names and burn them with a prayer of thanks for anything the angels have done. If there is no physical change, healing may have taken place at an emotional, mental or spiritual level. Have faith that the angels have done whatever is allowed under Spiritual Law.

CHAPTER TWENTY-EIGHT

Archangel Uriel

Archangel Uriel is the mighty Archangel who commands the Angels of Peace. His twin flame is Aurora and they work on the purple and gold ray, which is sometimes known as the ruby ray. Purple represents the power of transformation and forgiveness. It contains the violet of pure spirit with the red of action and so it stimulates the desire for spiritual service. Gold represents wisdom.

Uriel is the Archangel who looks after and develops the solar plexus chakra in humanity. At the third-dimensional level the solar plexus is yellow, which contains knowledge as well as holding your fears. The solar plexus is also a huge psychic receiver and transmitter. It is through this centre that you watch for danger, connect with your loved ones and tune into collective fears and catastrophes. This is why sensitive people often feel tense in this area.

Uriel is constantly helping you to develop this chakra from the yellow of knowledge to the golden level of wisdom. Then your fears from this life or another dissolve and you are untouched by the fears of those around you or in the collective. You connect to your soul's wisdom. After that his task is to help you expand this chakra so that you carry universal wisdom. Then you become a Wise One.

The sixth ray, to which Uriel is connected, is the ray of devotion and idealism. Its lowest expression is religious organisations and dogma, while the highest aspiration is pure spirituality, which accepts all religions and is beyond them.

Call on Uriel for insight, clarity and vision, especially to help you understand another's motives or hidden agenda.

Jesus Christ, or Sananda as he is known on the inner planes, also represents the sixth ray, which is indigo, and naturally Archangel Uriel and Sananda work in co-operation to develop qualities of grace, mercy and compassion in humanity. They offer loving protection and teach selfless service. They direct those who seek the tools to reach God by devotional service. They inspire brotherhood and sisterhood and promote togetherness and cooperation at all times.

> I receive hundreds of letters from people, many of them desperate, categorising all their fears, miseries and troubles. I was driving to teach a seminar one beautiful sunny day and was mulling this over, when Sananda came in and said, 'Do not indulge their misery, their negativity, their doubts and fears. Tell them to send you their hopes and dreams, their visions and intentions and my angels will empower and manifest them.'

The solar plexus is very strongly influenced by your thoughts. Yellow is the colour of thinking, the mind colour. The third eye is indigo, the colour of the sixth ray. As it develops and refines, the third eye chakra becomes white gold and finally crystal clear, while the solar plexus becomes gold.

Hazel Courteney, the alternative specialist and health writer, author of the fascinating book, *Divine Intervention*, was writing an article about my work and she kindly agreed to work with me. First we took her aura photograph, which was a beautiful pink, the colour of compassion and love. Then I linked in to her. Archangel Uriel entered and worked to move some past life fears from her solar plexus. After the session we took another aura photograph. Now her aura was filled with a spiritual blue colour and a deep gold light emerged from her solar plexus. Archangel Uriel had cleared old fears and replaced them with wisdom.

Thursday is the day Archangel Uriel's power is connected most strongly to Earth and is a good day to meditate on him or ask for his help.

You can ask him to help you renew your dedication to achieving goals in any area of life. Many business people are connected to him for this reason. Those who are in service, such as social workers, public servants, farmers, missionaries and idealistic lawyers, work under his umbrella. He is the guardian of writers.

Archangel Uriel's spiritual retreat is in the Tatra Mountains in Poland. I have found it most helpful to ask before I go to sleep to be taken there to have any fears removed. Whenever I do this, I dream about my past, which tells me that old energy is still held in my solar plexus.

The angels work in mysterious and fascinating ways. A friend, David, who is a businessman and spiritual Master, offered to help me create greater financial stability in my life and to master money. So I went to stay with him and his girlfriend for a weekend.

Before I went to bed, I asked Archangel Uriel to clear any financial fears that I still held within me, during sleep. In the morning I woke dreaming that black balls were being pulled out of the depths of my solar plexus and I knew something important was being released.

Later that day David and I drove to the beach to go for a walk. However, a dark cloud sat over the car, pouring rain on to us, and refused to move, although the sun was shining everywhere else. So we got out pen and paper and made plans. Then we asked the angels for a signal that these were right. An incredible thing happened.

On the way back to David's home, we pulled up at a set of traffic lights. At the same moment his brother pulled up next to us and stopped. They opened the car windows to shout 'Hello' and to David's amazement his brother threw an envelope containing £1,000 through the car window.

David was beaming from ear to ear. He said, 'I think that's a signal from the angels that abundance is on its way.'

Angels of Peace gather to pour their calming light on to angry eruptions all the time.

Petra told me that she was sitting quietly at home one day when a vision flashed in front of her of an angry crowd in Bosnia, during the time of the troubles. She found she was watching pictures as if on a television set. To her amazement she saw a white angel with wonderful wings put light round the crowd and try to soothe it.

She knew nothing about angels before that moment but after that she could not doubt their presence.

Service work

Every time you think with compassion of a person, place or situation in need of help, you create a bridge of light along which the angels can travel in order to help, if you ask them to.

Find a map of the world. Place a lighted candle on a place of conflict and direct Archangel Uriel and his Angels of Peace to enfold the situation and the people there in peace.

CHAPTER TWENTY-NINE

Uriel's Angels of Peace

Some years ago beautiful Angels of Peace approached me. They were luminous, creamy-white beings, with soft feathery wings. They stood about eight feet tall and emanated a sense of total peace and stillness.

They asked me to impart this message to those who would listen. *'Peace must be spread and it can only start within individuals who are ready to forgo their power struggle with others. Peace is surrender to spirit, not proving you are better than another.'*

Then they suggested that everyone be asked to make a corner of their home into a peace corner, a space in which you think only peaceful thoughts. It can be as small as one chair in the house, but having chosen the spot you should never approach it unless your thoughts are centred and peaceful. From that little corner peace will spread, filling and protecting your home. I describe fully what happened during the angels' visitation in *A Little Light on Angels*.

> The mother of a thirteen-year-old girl told me that she and her husband were in considerable conflict and their two sons quarrelled incessantly. Their young teenage daughter read my book and decided to create a peace corner. She chose a chair and sat in it every day, thinking

peaceful thoughts and asking the Angels of Peace to help her. Her mother said that the effect on the household was amazing. A balm spread through the family. Within a short space of time the boys had literally stopped quarrelling and become friends, while she and her husband had resolved all their difficulties.

She added that you could feel the peace as you walked into their house and now each of them took time to sit in the peace chair.

If you create a peace corner in your village or city, where you think peaceful thoughts as you pass, the Angels of Peace will be able to anchor peace at that point and everyone who walks through it will be touched. It is even more effective if you ask friends to do this with you.

You can ask the Angels of Peace for inner peace, to help you release fear and anger and to renew your hope when it is dimmed. They will help you to find practical resolutions to any problems in your relationships and assist all who serve others.

When you invoke Uriel and his Angels of Peace, they are able actively to promote peace where there is war, harmony where there is conflict and justice where there is injustice.

Like all Spiritual Beings of Light, the Angels of Peace are waiting and longing to help but cannot do so under Spiritual Law unless they are asked. A lady shared the following story during a phone-in.

Her beloved father had died and she was devastated. She did not know how she could cope with the funeral. When she went to bed, in desperation she asked the angels to help. That night an angel came into her dream and she heard hymns being sung around her. She felt total peace and this feeling stayed with her and sustained her through the funeral.

Angels often sing over you when you are asleep at night. If you ask them to they will do so more often. The music heals you and fills you with peace.

Many people have victim consciousness. They believe they are helpless and powerless and send this energy out so strongly that they indeed become victimised, miserable and oppressed. When you feel sorry for the victim, you disempower him. The energy of your thoughts and emotions weakens him.

If someone is cruel, a bully or a tyrant, they feel separate, unloved and bad about themselves. They disempower others in order to make themselves feel better. You sense when someone is angry or critical of you and automatically put up your shutters. This closes your heart and makes a loving relationship, or indeed any kind of change, impossible. Bullies are also sensitive to criticism and anger. They too close down their hearts when others judge them and change is blocked.

Bullies are unconsciously looking for and drawing to themselves people who will allow themselves to be

victimised and made to feel powerless. Victims are unconsciously seeking bullies in order to learn their lessons of empowerment. Each places himself in the perfect position to learn about self-worth, confidence, personal power and love.

This also happens on a global level. When we read about horror, fighting and oppression in the press and feel sorry for the downtrodden and angry with the perpetrator, mass judgement shuts down the possibility for change. Our collective energy is fuelling the problem.

A Master does not judge another's incarnation. He recognises that both sides are learning in the only way they know how. He looks beyond the personality struggles and visualizes them free from the shackles of conflict and oppression and invokes the angels to heal the situation. Then he looks at the glory of their God selves. Whatever you see in another you help bring into their life.

Nor does a Master stand back and watch someone being hurt or condone genocide. If someone is getting seriously damaged, he enters without judgement to protect the victim. Then he works to empower both victim and perpetrator.

Individually and collectively we have the power, with the help of the angels, to create peace on Earth.

To create a Peace Altar
Place a cloth on a small table or chest.

On it you may have a candle, incense, crystals, flowers, feathers, or pictures of loved ones to raise the vibration.

Find a beautiful bowl and place it on your altar. This is your angel bowl.

Lovingly write the names of anyone you wish the Angels of Peace to enfold in their wings.

Put the names in your angel bowl and know that the angels will help them.

Remove the names when you feel the time is right.

Service work
To create a Peace Corner
Choose a corner of your house where you only have thoughts of peace.

Invite the Angels of Peace to spread their energy through your home.

Create bridges of light by sending thoughts of peace to people, places and situations so that the angels have permission to bring peace there.

CHAPTER THIRTY

Archangel Zadkiel

The mighty Archangel Zadkiel commands the angels of mercy, joy and transmutation. He is often known as the Angel of Freedom.

His twin flame is Amethyst, the feminine aspect of the violet ray, which offers transmutation through forgiveness, compassion and mercy. The amethyst crystal represents the symbolic condensation of the violet ray and is the birthstone for Aquarius, the New Age.

When you invoke Archangel Zadkiel, he imbues you with the desire and power to free yourself from your negativity and limitation. If you express the desire to forgive yourself or others, the angels of the violet ray will intercede and purify the cause of the problem, thus releasing all karma. Call on his energy for more tolerance or to help you be diplomatic in difficult circumstances. He transmutes lower consciousness into higher. When this happens you are free and ready to express the joy of life.

The day on which his ray is most powerfully felt on Earth is Saturday.

Zadkiel and Amethyst are the angels of the seventh ray of ceremonial order and magic. It is the ray which grounds spirituality into the physical, bringing heaven to Earth.

An unevolved being on this ray would be superstitious, bigoted, proud and narrow-minded. Someone working with the higher aspect is developing strength, self-reliance, an expanded mind, tolerance and the ability to work in harmony with God. This is the ray of leaders, diplomats and royalty.

> One of the lightest and most joyous Angel Workshops I ever facilitated was in Ireland. So many Irish people are psychic and several said to me that the Angels of Joy had come on to the stage with me and had been playing with me during the day.

The spiritual retreat of Archangel Zadkiel is in Cuba. The chakra he is working to expand for humanity is the seat of the soul chakra, which is above the head and links you to your higher self or soul. He is helping everyone on the planet to ascend by waking up each individual and connecting them to their soul energy.

Archangel Zadkiel is working in alignment with St Germain, the Chohan of the seventh ray. At the Harmonic Convergence so many of us meditated and prayed for the raising of consciousness on the planet that we created a huge light. This enabled St Germain to apply to Source for a dispensation to help us. God granted us the Violet Flame of Transmutation, which dissolves negative vibrations if called upon to do so. Anyone can use this and all you have to do is ask for it to come to you.

The Violet Flame is so powerful that many have used it to heal their physical bodies, their emotions,

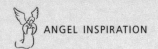

relationships, beliefs and deep soul-level problems. It literally burns into the source of the blockage and transmutes the heavy vibration into light.

Because so many people have raised their consciousness, the Silver Ray of Grace and Harmony merged recently with the Violet Flame to create the Silver Violet Flame of Grace and Transmutation. The Flame has expanded to include a range of vibrations from pale lilac, mauve and silver through to deep violet.

As soon as you work with the Silver Violet Flame the colour violet starts to form in your aura and you radiate on a higher spiritual vibration. At one workshop we were doing exercises to transmute problems and send the Silver Violet Flame to situations and people in the world. One participant went out in the lunch-break to have her aura photographed. Her entire aura was filled with a wonderful vibrant violet. She said that her previous aura photographs had always been yellow or red. Yellow is the energy of thinking, and working logically. Red is the adrenaline of stress.

The exercises that we did in the workshop will have affected her aura for a short time. However, if you decide to work constantly with the Silver Violet Flame and other higher energies, the spiritual colours will be a permanent part of your auric field. Then you will naturally attract higher people and situations into your life.

When I started to call in the angels of the Violet Flame, people kept saying they thought for a moment that I had a violet rinse in my hair. They were seeing their light around me.

It helps if you can visualise violet, mauve, silver and lilac flames surrounding whatever you want to purify.

You may use it to transmute anger and any negative emotions you are feeling, to purify a relationship or events from your childhood or past incarnations.

> Two very elderly sisters were involved in a conflict which had lasted several decades. They hated each other. One became bedridden, living in a nursing home. She appeared to have no reason to hold on to life, but hatred forms a deep cord and her family knew that she and her sister were holding on to each other. Although they had not met for years, she could not pass over until her physical body deteriorated or the cord was transmuted.
>
> The daughter of one of them pictured the two old ladies within the Silver Violet Flame until the energy of hatred was transmuted and the older sister was able to return home to God.

You can invoke the Silver Violet Flame to blaze a path in front of you during the day, so that all you are about to experience is cleansed. This ensures that you handle the events of the day with the highest integrity and do not get contaminated by other people's energy.

You can even call it into parts of your body where you hold physical blocks. It has tremendous power to release and heal. I was walking along a clifftop one day invoking the Silver Violet Flame. From time to time I thought of a friend who was in hospital having a lump in her breast removed. I pictured the Violet Flame going into her breast.

When I spoke to her on the phone, she said she kept seeing violet light all round her. The doctor told her

they had caught it just in time and she was absolutely fine.

As you affirm I AM you are declaring that your God self is in alignment with that quality or person. Here is a very powerful I AM affirmation which was given to me by Archangel Zadkiel and it will help you to identify totally with the Silver Violet Flame.

I AM the Silver Violet Flame
I AM the Flame of Mercy
I AM the Flame of Joy
I AM the Flame of Transmutation
I AM St Germain
I AM Archangel Zadkiel.

As you say 'I AM St Germain', 'I AM Archangel Zadkiel', you are affirming that your God Self now identifies totally with St Germain and Archangel Zadkiel and merges with their energy so that you can express it in your life.

When you affirm this with energy and force, you will observe your life changing as all your conscious or unconscious negativity is transmuted and grace enters.

Service work
You can do this during meditation or even when you are walking, or standing in a queue.

Invoke the Silver Violet Flame. Imagine, sense or visualise the flame surrounding you and consuming all your lower vibrations.

Picture a person, place or situation where there is

disharmony and surround it with the Silver Violet Flame until it feels purified.

Imagine the Silver Violet Flame surrounding the whole planet and burning up the dross.

Conclude by affirming 'I AM the Silver Violet Flame' as often as you can.

CHAPTER THIRTY-ONE

Archangels Release Vows

When you make a vow at a ceremony, whether it is of marriage, confirmation or to enter any religion, sect or brotherhood, angels come together to help keep you to your vow. If you are baptised as a baby, the vow is taken on your behalf, and angels are assigned to keep you on that path.

When children play 'marriage vows' and create a ceremony, if the energy is right, angels will respond and the promise will be treated as a sacred vow. At a spiritual level those children are bound. On a few occasions people have realised that they played at weddings when they were children. Usually, for the impact to be binding, it was with a special friend. Often the children's vow was made with others attending, which heightens the energy of the dedication. I remember one woman who was reluctant to marry and when the childhood vow was released she felt free to marry her partner.

Pacts entered into with ritual are also in this category. So are oaths of allegiance and some contracts that you undertake.

Time has speeded up now and humans are living several lifetimes in one, without severing the vows to their previous marriages, religions or career contracts. A marriage is a ceremony. A divorce is a signed piece of paper, which does not release the energy of the original contract. This means that many people are held back by outdated psychic cords, which the angels maintain.

It is important to release these vows, contracts and dedications and free yourself to live fully.

In past lives you may have taken vows of chastity, poverty, obedience or silence. Many people took vows of fidelity and charity by which you have to give everything away. Other vows are of austerity, conformity or penitence. If you do not fully release the vows at death, they will influence your current life.

If someone has cursed you in this life or another, that curse will be locked into your energy system. Of course, a curse made with ritual, such as the sticking in of pins, is extremely malevolent to receiver and giver. However, please watch your thoughts and words. When you curse someone who has robbed or violated you, you are tied to that person through lifetimes until it is released. Mothers and fathers who curse an unborn child that they don't want, put a block on that soul. It is much more easily done than people realise, especially if you are angry or in an emotional state at the time. It is wasted energy to feel guilty. Far better to release the curse or damnation and forgive yourself.

An implant of any nature is a kind of curse. It ties you to the energy of the person who implanted it and condemns you both. Aliens sometimes place implants in humans as they learn from our mental, emotional, sexual and physical bodies, which are different from theirs. These need to be removed. In Atlantis, when the vibration lowered and humans misused technology to gain power over others, control boxes were placed in slaves, which could be operated by their masters. If you were

a controller or a slave, you will still be tied in some way and your consciousness will be affected.

The angels and Ascended Masters are very happy to help with the release of any vows, dedications, contracts and curses from your energy systems. You may particularly like to invoke the following mighty and powerful Beings.

Lord Kumeka, Master of Light and Chohan of the eighth ray of cleansing, which is aquamarine, is very powerful when invoked.

Vywamus, who is the Higher Self of Sanat Kumara, the Being in charge of your ascension process, is a mighty power to call on.

Djwhal Kuhl, who works with Lord Kuthumi, Chohan of the second ray, and brought through the Alice Bailey books, is dedicated to helping all on this planet.

Archangel Michael and his hosts of angels has the authority to release and transmute all dark energy.

One way of doing this is to make a decree. An affirmation is repeated to impress your unconscious mind. A decree is much more powerful. It is a command to the Universe, taken from a point of mastery. You make it once. It is so powerful that the forces of the Universe must respond.

To make your decree, sit or stand with your shoulders back and your head up. It must be spoken aloud with authority.

A preamble such as the following is very helpful to clear the energy around you.

Preamble to decree
I forgive all those who have ever hurt, harmed or cursed me, known and unknown, as I ask for forgiveness of those who I have hurt, harmed or cursed, known and unknown.

I invoke the Law of Forgiveness, under Grace, for all situations, conditions and events in my life and all past lives.

Invocation
I now invoke Lord Kumeka, Chohan of the eighth ray, Vywamus, Djwhal Kuhl and the mighty Archangel Michael to release outdated vows.

Decree
In the name of God and all that is light, under the Law of Grace, I now decree that all vows, curses, pacts, dedications and implants made by me or to me are rescinded and transmuted, whether in this life or another, in all parallel lives and Universes, in all my bodies. I command that the angels who administer these vows release their duties forthwith. I AM totally free.

Repeat this three times.

It is done.

It is also very powerful to hold a releasing meditation and ceremony. See page 219.

Service work
Decree for the release of vows and curses which tie families, countries and humanity as a whole.

Example: In the name of God and all that is light, under Grace, I now decree that all vows, curses, pacts

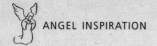

and dedications which hold back (name of family, town or country) be rescinded. I command that the angels who administer these vows release their duties forthwith.

Repeat this three times.

It is done.

CHAPTER THIRTY-TWO

Your Expanded Self

You are greater than you believe you are. The part of you on Earth is a fraction of your soul. Many of you are great Masters on the inner planes and your life mission can be greatly expanded when you totally identify with your true self.

I do not allow just anyone to enter my energy fields. It is a very personal thing for someone to give you healing, massage or do any form of energy work on your body.

However, when I met Susie Anthony and she offered me a session of her special healing I jumped at the opportunity. I felt wonderful when she finished.

She told me that a spirit guide had been working with her throughout the session. He was a thirty-three-level Master and an incredibly powerful and mighty being.

She then described him in detail, his physical appearance as well as his connections to places and his mission. I was astounded. She was describing a close friend! I laughed and said, 'That's not a spirit guide. That's a friend.' She retuned and agreed, saying. 'He is an incredibly evolved Master on the inner planes but he does not know who he is on Earth.'

Interestingly, I twice had flashes of his 'golden body' and on each occasion had told him that he was a mighty Master. It transpired that other channels had also told him this. At last I think he is beginning to have an inkling of who he truly is.

You too may be a highly evolved Master in the inner planes. As you identify with your true self, you can manifest your power and light on Earth.

Catherine also experienced her expanded self. When she reached adulthood, an angel by the name of Aqua la A Wa La appeared to her. The angel told her that she was here to heal oceans and emotions. She added, 'The colour aquamarine entered my Being in my vast state and expanded my consciousness in such a way that I also had my feet deep in the Earth and my head in galaxies.'

It appears that her personal mission on Earth is healing, whilst the mission of her mighty soul is to heal the oceans and emotions.

Aqua means water, the element of the emotions. And marine, of course, is sea or ocean. How perfect that the colour aquamarine filled her.

Catherine Seiler sent me these extracts from her diary, which add intriguing insights about the greater selves and the multi-dimensional lives we lead. Many star children, those from other galaxies and universes, are incarnating on Earth now to help with the great shift in consciousness taking place here.

I was also delighted to read her letter, for my guide, Kumeka, said that Archangel Metatron works mainly in another Universe. There are twelve Universes and I write about this in *A Little Light on Ascension*.

Catherine's diary starts after an incredible angel meditation. 'On the way home I saw a large angel, I believe it to be Metatron. After seeing him, a voice came into my head, and told me I was a Star Person, to which I replied, "Yeah, sure."

'While lying in bed, I was told that I came from a technically superior race of beings, but inferior in the sense of spirituality and emotions. I had agreed to come to the planet Earth to experience these things and report them back to the Council on Urr. Seemingly I have been doing this every evening, but obviously cannot remember much, except vague images.

'This will explain why Metatron came to speak to me, as he is the angel that works mostly in that Universe, and why he wants to work with me on Planet Earth. The planet is also called the Blue Planet, which is why I get so much comfort from the colour blue.

'This morning I closed my eyes, and saw bright pin-pricks of light. I was told they were stars and planets from my home solar system, called Gamita.

'I understand much from my other planet but as yet do not know how to translate this into the language I understand on Earth.

'I must also add that on my way to church on Sunday, I was told that Gamita was from the eleventh Universe and that, as I mentioned before, Gamita is in the seventh quadrant of that Universe. I know I should understand all this, but with all the difficulties of planet Earth, I am more than a little tired at present.'

I also received a letter from Suzanne, which relates her experience of her expanded self.

Suzanne was feeling stressed and unsettled during an interconnecting flight between Muscat and Abu Dhabi. She tried to relax and visualise a calming scene. She writes: 'Then the scene seemed to take off on its own, became no longer something over which I had control.

'My mind expanded out towards the stars, opened out to Space and a knowing that there was intelligent, cultured, wise life out there. The feeling of space filled my mind completely – or rather, my mind suddenly had no boundaries, expanded beyond the confines of my skull. The senses of my body drifted away and I no longer heard the gabble on the plane. But I did not feel as if I was asleep. I was still aware somehow of being on the plane.

'My consciousness was within an enormous, peaceful, ultramarine darkness. Down below I saw a small dark figure standing within a lighter area, as if illumined by a shaft of light. I wondered what it was and it came into my mind, as if there were presences in the ultramarine darkness communicating it to me, that this was the frightened core of myself. It seemed tiny and distant now, but in waking life on earth it often takes up the whole of me. It was a skinny, black, slimy-skinned and nervy, hot creature. It squirmed a lot, looking back and up over its shoulder at us though it could not see anything in the dark above it. I say "us" because I felt I was in the company of more than one other presence. I also felt these other presences to be very compassionate and caring.

'"Why is it so frightened?" I asked.

'"Because it has been brought up on ignorance," came the answer from the ultramarine darkness. "It doesn't *know* anything."

'"Poor thing," I thought. I pitied it and felt kindly towards it.

'Then my bodily senses felt the plane begin the descent into Abu Dhabi. I did not want to leave the stars and this expansive ultramarine place. I thought, "No! I don't want to go back down to Earth, don't want to leave or lose this feeling of Space."

'"Don't think of Earth as down," the compassionate presences said. "Earth is part of it all."

'And suddenly I felt I understood the infinity and realised that Earth was not down, not separate from the stars. And I got the feeling that we were coming in to land at just another spaceport. I came back properly to my senses, feeling very relaxed and with a wonderful feeling of having been cared for by those other presences.'

Later Suzanne wrote in her diary. 'The feeling of the "vision" being more than mere daydream persisted for some time afterwards. I would go up on to the moorland behind our cottage and stare up at the sky feeling there were companions, caring presences there. But I've got a sceptical side which tries to explain things away and after a while the experience got relegated to merely a memory.'

She adds a postscript: 'And ten years on, I feel I can no longer deny the reality of these experiences!'

So many of us are Great Masters, unbeknown. Many people tell me that when they see the pictures of the Ascended Masters on my website, they recognise them as people who come into their dreams and talk to them. Ascended Masters are our older brothers. They do not think they are superior to us any more than you think you are superior to your younger brother, just older.

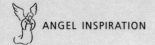

Service work

You may already be a great and wise Ascended Being. Act as if you are and your light will touch everyone you meet.

In meditation go out into the stars and connect to the other planets, galaxies and Universes, taking love from planet Earth.

CHAPTER THIRTY-THREE

Archangels and the Chakras

Each of the Archangels of the first seven rays, and his twin flame, is in charge of the development of one of the chakras, as follows. A chakra is a spiritual energy centre and there are seven main ones.

Animals have only one chakra. The base chakra in humans has differentiated into the base and sacral.

Base and sacral chakra	Archangel Gabriel and Hope
Solar plexus chakra	Archangel Uriel and Aurora
Heart chakra	Archangel Chamuel and Charity
Throat chakra	Archangel Michael and Faith
Third-eye chakra	Archangel Raphael and Mary
Crown chakra	Archangel Jophiel and Christine
Seat of the soul chakra	Archangel Zadkiel and Amethyst

When you walk the worldly path, your thoughts, words, intentions and actions are vibrating within a particular frequency band. You are operating within the third-dimensional frequency. The third-dimensional chakras are anchored within your etheric body, which is the body's counterpart in the ethers. You are known as a third-dimensional human and your higher chakras reach up to your Higher Self or soul for instructions.

The third-dimensional chakras are:

1. Base	Red	Survival
2. Sacral	Orange	Emotions and sexuality
3. Solar plexus	Yellow	Personal power
4. Heart	Green	Personal and emotional love
5. Throat	Turquoise	Communication and trust
6. Third eye	Indigo	Higher mental powers and healing
7. Crown	Violet	Reaching to your soul
8. Seat of the soul	Blue white	Connection with your soul

The chakras are in place above and below you, like an extending ladder. As you raise your consciousness your thoughts, words, intentions and actions vibrate at a higher level. The third-dimensional chakras move down your legs. New chakras, which vibrate at a higher level, within the fourth-dimensional frequency band, move down and take their place. When these are anchored and activated you become a fourth-dimensional human and walk the path of detachment and love. When the highest of these, the white violet crown chakra, is active, your soul or Higher Self merges with your personality. You then take your instructions from your Monad or I AM Presence, which was your original spark from Source. Your Monad is your true God essence and your aim is to bring this divine aspect of yourself into your physical life.

The fourth-dimensional chakras are:

9. Base	Pearl-white	Joy
10. Sacral	Pale pink-orange	Balance of masculine and feminine
11. Solar plexus	Gold	Wisdom
12. Heart	Pale violet-pink	Unconditional love
13. Throat	Deep blue violet	Psychic and spiritual powers
14. Third eye	Golden-white	Divine thought
15. Crown	White-violet	Take instruction from Monad which is your true divine self

When you anchor and activate the ninth chakra, the base chakra, your life is based in joy. You increase your spiritual responsibilities and at a galactic level you become a guardian of the Earth.

Your tenth chakra becomes active when you balance your masculine and feminine energy, so that you can support yourself, think clearly, rationalise, defend yourself and at the same time bring forward creative ideas, nurture and heal yourself and listen to your wisdom. This wholeness is a state of alignment with the soul and enables you to reach into the solar system to access information of a higher nature.

The activation of the gold chakra of wisdom in your solar plexus enables you to meditate in groups to link into other galaxies. You become an ambassador for Earth.

When the violet-pink energy enters the heart, a spiritualisation of the heart takes place. On a cosmic level this links you to the rest of the Universe.

The deep blue violet of the throat chakra enables you to communicate with Archangels and higher beings, to materialise and dematerialise as well as to start learning to bilocate and use higher powers.

When the fourteenth chakra, which is golden-white, opens, your mind surrenders to the divine plan. You communicate with the Masters and higher guides.

As the crown chakra opens, your soul and personality merge and you radiate white violet light upwards and take instructions directly from your Monad.

When the fifth-dimensional chakras move into your aura, the third-dimensional ones move down into the Earth and the fourth-dimensional ones down into your legs.

The fifth-dimensional chakras are:

16. Base	Platinum	Bliss. Life based in spiritual service
17. Sacral	Magenta and platinum	The divine feminine
18. Solar plexus	Gold and rainbow	Universal wisdom
19. Heart	Pure white	Christ consciousness
20. Throat	Royal blue	Co-creation with God
21. Third eye and		
22. Crown merge	Crystal	Merge with Monad

You can call yourself an Ascended Master when the fifth-dimensional base chakra is anchored and activated. You start to take instructions from your Monad. You start to walk the Christ path on Earth. And there are still many initiations to undertake as you move up the spiritual ladder.

Only when all the fifth-dimensional chakras are anchored and activated are you a fully Ascended Master. Most elect to remain on Earth in service to humanity, taking instruction directly from God. Very few people have achieved this in the past but we are now in an incredible window of opportunity when the angelic hierarchy and great Beings of Light are helping those who wish to dedicate their lives to ascension to achieve this possibility.

You may also prepare yourself for higher service by anchoring in meditation the next fifty chakras into your aura.

You are a multi-dimensional being and your chakras will automatically open according to your frequency. The more time and energy you spend in identifying yourself with the higher chakras, the more your life will be lived at a higher level. You will attract higher-vibration people and situations, which will enable you to reach ascension and bring others to ascension more quickly.

Service work

The greatest service work you can offer is to anchor and activate your own higher chakras so that you radiate great light.

You can also teach those who are ready how to do this, using the exercises in this book.

Angel Exercises

and

Meditations

Connect with Your Guardian Angel

Your Guardian Angel is always with you, sending love, compassion and encouragement to you. It is really helpful to know your angel's name.

You can ask your Guardian Angel for help, for support and comfort, or to talk to someone else through their angel. Gold is the angelic colour and it helps your angel to connect more easily with you when you sense, think or visualize that colour around you. Sometimes people do not receive their angel's name because they are trying too hard or thinking too much. Relax and try again another time or ask your angel to impress its name upon you when you wake in the morning. A name is a vibration and your angel's name may be simple, complex, ordinary or unusual. If you are given the name of an Archangel, your angel is most likely an angel working under the direction of that Archangel. Just accept your first impression.

Meditation to connect with your angel and find his name

1. Make sure you are in a place where you will be undisturbed.
2. If possible, raise the energy with flowers, a candle, incense, angelic music if you like it and beautiful objects or books.

3. Sit or lie with your back straight.

4. Ground yourself by imagining roots reaching down from your feet into the Earth.

5. Place a golden egg of protection around you. Take a few minutes to breathe the colour gold into it, relaxing your body as you do this.

6. Mentally ask your Guardian Angel to step into your aura and touch you. Expect a physical sensation, or a fragrance, or a feeling of great love.

7. Ask your angel to put his wings around you and hold you. Relax into this.

8. Ask your Guardian Angel's name. Accept the first name that comes to you.

9. Calmly ask for any help you need.

10. Thank your Guardian Angel.

11. Open your eyes and stretch.

Angel Wings

As you grow and develop spiritually, you manifest and radiate angelic qualities. When this happens you grow angel wings. These do not appear physically, of course, though you may feel pain, tension, tingling or a sensation behind your shoulders when the energy is starting to gather.

The wings appear in your etheric body, which is the invisible spiritual counterpart to your physical body, where your history and development are recorded. For example, if you have had a limb amputated, you will still have that limb in your etheric body and you may feel sensations in it, which will seem to you to be physical sensations.

Everyone's wings are different. They will have a variety of shapes, colours, textures and qualities. Some people have tiny little fast-beating wings. Others have huge, feathery ones. Some are gossamer-soft, others strong and powerful. They can be pointed, rounded or any shape. Your wings may be transparent, pink, white, gold or any other colour.

It is wonderful to know what your wings are like and to feel or sense them. And your wings change, develop and become bigger and stronger all the time, so this is a meditation you can do from time to time to sense how your wings are reflecting your angelic qualities.

Some people seem to have double wings or two sets as they expand their consciousness.

Meditation for your angel wings

1. Make sure you are in a place where you will be un-disturbed.
2. If possible, raise the energy with flowers, a candle, appropriate music if you like it and beautiful objects or books.
3. Sit or lie with your back straight.
4. Ground yourself by imagining roots reaching down from your feet into the Earth.
5. Relax and let go of the outside world. Focus on your breathing and when you feel comfortable, stroke your body with your breath from your head down. Imagine each breath is making you feel more relaxed and peaceful.
6. Be aware of your spine and notice from which part your wings unfurl.
7. Let your wings spread out fully.
8. Sense their size, shape, texture and colour.
9. Gently and slowly imagine yourself moving your wings until you can flap them easily.
10. Ask your angels to hold your hands and help you to fly out into the sky. Enjoy flying with their support.
11. When you are ready, let go of their hands and fly through the stars. Experience the joy and freedom of your angelic self.
12. Drop golden angel dust on people and places who need it.

13. Return to your body and sit quietly for a few moments.
14. Feel your feet on the Earth and make sure you are grounded.
15. Stretch and open your eyes.
16. Congratulate yourself on receiving your angel wings.

Meet the Angel of Your Home or Workplace

Every home, office, hospital, school or even government building has its own angel looking after it. When the energy is low, the angels have a very difficult task, and you can help them by raising it.

Each time you walk into a shop, sports centre, office block, someone's home or any kind of building, you affect the energy there. When you are feeling angry, fearful or unwell, you bring negativity with you, which makes it more difficult for the angel of the building to touch people and situations. When you are feeling bright, happy, loving and peaceful you bring a radiant light, which makes it easier for the angel to help everyone in the place. If you walk in and bless the building, that adds a great light and you receive blessings in your turn. If you ohm, even if it is a silent ohm, you start to clear and cleanse the place.

Obviously it is easier to connect with the angel of your home or workplace if the energy of the building is light and clear.

Meditation to meet the angel of your home or workplace

1. Make sure you are in a place where you will be undisturbed.
2. If possible, raise the energy with flowers, a candle, appropriate angelic music if you like it and beautiful objects or books.
3. Sit or lie with your back straight.
4. Ground yourself by imagining roots reaching down from your feet into the Earth.
5. Surround yourself in a protective golden egg of light.
6. Relax and let go of the outside world.
7. Quietly chant the ohm, pronounced 'ah-oh-mm', for a few minutes. If you cannot sound this aloud, do it silently.
8. Imagine the room you are in being filled with golden light.
9. Ask the angel of your home or workplace to appear to you. You may see, sense, feel or intuit his presence.
10. Send the angel your love and gratitude for looking after your home or the building you are in.
11. Open yourself to receive love and gratitude from this angel.
12. Ask for any message or how you can help the angel do his task more effectively. You may receive a visual or telepathic impression. You may even hear a response.
13. Sit quietly for a few minutes.
14. Then move your feet and hands. Stretch and open your eyes.

Fill Your Home with Angels

You decide on the energy of your home. No one influences you unless you allow them to. If your aura is weak or broken because you have given your power to someone or something, start immediately to strengthen it by eating good food, making strong affirmations, taking positive decisions, visualising what you want to happen, exercising and connecting to the angelic hierarchy of light.

Every time you think or talk about an angel, Archangel or Master, you draw some of their energy into your aura and make it more radiant.

When you have a strong, clear aura, other people will follow your visions and decisions.

To purify your home
To make your home welcoming to the angels, first clear out all the rubbish. Tidy the space. Vacuum and clean the house. Redecorate it if necessary.

Open the windows to let stale energy out and fresh air into your home. If you or someone else has had a quarrel or said nasty things, this is an essential step.

Cleanse the space by lighting incense and wafting it into each corner. Use cymbals or bells in each of the rooms. Clap to break up stuck energy.

Check your bookshelves and throw away or recycle

any low-vibration books, which emit dark radiations. Plants with small leaves, such as ferns, transmute negative forms.

Call in the Silver Violet Flame and visualise it filling your home.

To raise light in your home
Buy or borrow spiritual books which radiate light. The pictures on your walls send out energy. Beautiful pictures of landscapes and seascapes, radiant or holy people, vital and alive children and animals, all pour out light.

Angels love colour, so brighten your home with coloured cushions or throws or rugs if needed. Fill your home with plants and flowers.

Make an altar in your home and place candles, crystals, beautiful objects and pictures or statues of saints and Ascended Masters on it. If you take a few moments each day to light the candle and say a prayer, this will attract an angel.

Meditate and pray. Dancing with joy lights up your home.

The sounds loved by angels
Classical music and much of the beautiful New Age music written to bring peace and harmony delights and attracts the angels. So does the playing of crystal or Tibetan bowls.

Angels love laughter. Fill your home with happy, laughing family and friends and the angels will come. Every time you sing beautiful or sacred songs, or chant, you make your home attractive. Chant the names of God, mantras and sound the ohm or aah. Hum happily.

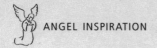

Spiritual conversations and saying good and loving things about people is melody to the higher beings.

Meditation to draw angels into your home

1. Make sure you are in a room where you will be undisturbed.
2. If possible, raise the energy with flowers, a candle, angelic music if you like it and beautiful objects or books.
3. Sit or lie with your back straight.
4. Ground yourself by imagining roots reaching down from your feet into the Earth.
5. Relax and let go of the outside world. Look around your home and bless all the beautiful things and people in it.
6. Close your eyes and visualise your home filled with beautiful golden light.
7. Ask for a column of golden light to come down from Source through your home into the Earth. Visualise it coming in.
8. Invoke angels to fill your home.
9. Trust that they have entered and experience what this feels like.
10. Thank them for coming and promise that you will keep the energy light and pure so that they continue to surround you.

Writing to Your Angel

One of the most effective ways of communicating with your Guardian Angel is by writing to him. You can also receive a reply!

You can do this anywhere at any time when you can be quiet or undisturbed. The principles are the same as those when writing to anyone. You think about the person you are writing to. You think about what you wish to communicate. Then you commit it to paper.

When you receive a reply from your angel, it is helpful to let go of thoughts and expectations. Just relax and let your hand write. You may be amazed and delighted by the responses you receive. Frequently people are offered profound wisdom, guidance and support in letters received from their angels, which could only come from a higher angelic source.

Do not write, 'I want this' or 'I want that'. Instead, explain the situation, so that your angel can help you in the highest way. Your explanation will also let the angel know just how much he can assist you, under Spiritual Law.

Angels will only ever write lovingly to you. If anything else comes through, you are not in touch with your angel. Close down.

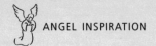

To write to your angel

1. Ground yourself by visualising roots going down into the Earth from your feet or the base of your spine.
2. Let yourself relax and become quiet and still.
3. Imagine yourself in a beautiful temple or somewhere where you feel at peace.
4. Think about your angel.
5. Write the date on your piece of paper, then 'Dear Angel' or whatever greeting you prefer.
6. Write your letter to your angel.
7. Thank him for his help.
8. Sign your letter.
9. Sit quietly.

To receive a reply from your angel

1. Take a fresh piece of paper and write the date at the top.
2. Relax for a moment.
3. Tell your angel you are ready to receive a reply.
4. Write a greeting at the top with your name. This may be 'Dear . . .'. Or you may find you have written a greeting you do not normally use. Angels often call you 'Beloved'.
5. Just let your pen or pencil flow. Do not check or censor anything with your mind. Let it come through your heart.
6. Let the angel sign off in any way he wishes.
7. Read your reply!

Writing to Someone Else's Angel

Another very important way of healing your life is to write to someone else's angel. There may be someone you would like to communicate with but cannot. If you find it difficult to express your feelings to that person or would like the relationship to move into a higher, clearer or more loving expression, tell that person's angel about it and ask for his help. Write about the circumstances and how you feel. Explain your anger, hurt, fear or love, admiration and affection to their angel. You may want to tell the angel that you would like help in releasing the past. You may want to bring the relationship to a solid level of friendship. Perhaps you would like to work with this person or would like to become closer. You may even want to offer help and support which the other refuses at the moment. Write and tell the angel.

Their angel will only act for their highest good. However, it is always in the highest good to heal relationships and promote friendship. The angel may even reply to you with insights you were unaware of before.

You can do this anywhere at any time when you can be quiet or undisturbed. The principles are the same as those in the previous exercise. You think about the person you are writing to. You think about what you wish to communicate. Then you commit it to paper.

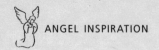

When you receive a reply from their angel, it is helpful to let go of thoughts and expectations. Just relax and let your hand write.

Do not write, 'I want this or that from the other person'. Explain the situation, so that their angel can help you in the highest way.

Angels will only ever write lovingly to you. If anything else comes through, you are not in touch with your angel. Close down.

To write to someone else's angel

1. Ground yourself by visualising roots going down into the Earth from your feet or the base of your spine.
2. Let yourself relax and become quiet and still.
3. Place a ball of reflecting white light around you.
4. Imagine yourself in a beautiful temple or somewhere where you feel at peace.
5. Think about the other person and their angel.
6. Write the date on your piece of paper, then 'Dear So and So's Angel' or whatever greeting you prefer.
7. Write your letter to their angel.
8. Thank them for their help.
9. Sign your letter.
10. Sit quietly.

To receive a reply from the other person's angel

1. Take a fresh piece of paper and write the date at the top.
2. Relax for a moment.
3. Tell their angel you are ready to receive a reply.

4. Write a greeting at the top with your name. This may be 'Dear . . .'. Or you may find you have written a greeting you do not normally use. Angels often call you 'Beloved'.
5. Just let your pen or pencil flow. Do not check or censor anything with your mind. Let it come through your heart.
6. Let the angel sign off in any way he wishes.
7. Read your reply!

Angel Invocation

Call in each of these energies one at a time, silently or aloud, and wait a moment until you feel each is anchored. This will increase your light greatly and the angels will touch you. You may of course add any angelic beings you wish to.

This is even more powerful if one person reads it aloud for a group.

Sit in a receptive position with your heart open and your palms up as you make the invocation.

I now invoke:
1. A pillar of golden light to surround me.
2. An angelic light shower.
3. A shower of angel love.
4. Angels to polish each facet of my soul diamond.
5. Archangel Michael to fill me with courage, positive results and protection.
6. Archangel Jophiel to bring me wisdom and illumination, tact and foresight.
7. Archangel Chamuel to expand the flame of love in my heart.
8. Archangel Gabriel for purification and guidance and to help me find forgiveness for myself and others.
9. Archangel Raphael to enhance my inner vision and for healing and abundance.

10. Archangel Uriel for peace and to free me from my mental and emotional chains.
11. Archangel Zadkiel to bring me mercy and transmute my energy.
12. Archangel Metatron to increase my light levels to the maximum I can carry.
13. Mother Mary to heal my inner child and fill me with compassion.
14. The Lords of Karma, The Great Divine Director, The Goddess of Liberty, Lady Nada, Pallas Athena, Elohim Vista, Kwan Yin, Portia, for mercy and release of karma.

When you have finished your invocation, surround yourself in a protective ball of pure white radiant light.

Angel Invocation for the Planet

This is an invocation to send armies of angels to help the planet.

Call in each of these energies one at a time, silently or aloud, and wait a moment until you feel each is anchored. Then mentally visualise millions of angels streaming across rainbow bridges of light to do your bidding. This is even more powerful if a group of people make this invocation together.

It is more focused if you name the particular places or group of people to which you wish to direct the angels. Sit in a receptive position with your heart open and your palms up as you make the invocation.

I now invoke:
1. The angels of peace and direct them to the Congo (or name any person or place where they are particularly needed).
2. The angels of abundance and I direct them to places of poverty.
3. The angels of compassion to enfold those with broken hearts and hurts.
4. The angels of healing to touch those in pain.
5. The angels of cooperation where there is disagreement.

6. The angels of openness to unlock minds and hearts where there is secrecy or dogma.

7. The angels of clarity to bring light where there is confusion.

8. The angels of power to support those who lack confidence.

9. The angels of freedom to release mental or physical chains.

10. The angels of tenderness to soften those who are hard-hearted.

11. The angels of education to illuminate the minds of those who are ready to learn.

12. The angels of joy to bring laughter where there is sadness.

13. The angels of hope to bring light to the oppressed.

14. The angels of creativity where solutions are needed.

15. The angels of humour and play to lighten the serious.

16. The angels of courage and strength to arm those who are spiritual warriors.

Channelling the Angels

Imagine a telephone line. You can talk to the person on the other end if the conditions are right. However, if they are not, the line may be too crackly to be able to hear what the other person is telling you.

Channelling means raising your frequency to that of your angel, so that you can communicate with him and receive information from him directly.

There is always a direct line between you and your angel, so you can connect as long as the frequency is right. Many people have channelled guides, angels and even Ascended Masters without being aware that they are doing so.

If you have ever heard yourself uttering words of wisdom and thought, 'Where on Earth did that come from?' it was probably your angel talking through you.

If you have found yourself writing or typing fluently and been amazed at the speed, creativity and quality of what you have done, then you were channelling your angel. It happens all the time and you can practise allowing it to happen consciously.

Make yourself relaxed, still, serene and centred. That is the way to clear the distortion from the line. Then raise your consciousness by forgiveness and non-judgement to a higher level. Appreciation, joy, love and beauty also raise your consciousness.

Obviously you cannot channel your angel if you are totally closed down and sceptical. Even if you are a creative genius with a constant unconscious connection, doubt will close down the channel when you try to connect consciously. So you need to be open, intuitive, receptive and relaxed.

Channelling your angel is most effective when you use both sides of your brain in cooperation. You need the left-brain abilities of focus and concentration as well as right-brain creativity, intuition and openness.

Your desire and intent is most important. If you are trying to test the oracle, your angel will not respond. If, however, you genuinely wish to make a close link to your higher guidance and intend to listen to it, your angel will be more than delighted to give you information, help, guidance, encouragement and inspiration.

It is a good idea to foster a close relationship with your Guardian Angel before you try to communicate with other angels and even with the Archangels and Ascended Masters. This too will happen as you raise your frequency and become more experienced.

Because your Guardian Angel's energy is so familiar to you, you may not realise that you are receiving information from that source. You may well feel that it is simply your own thoughts. I always feel that there is a golden quality when the angels speak. Remember that they will only ever speak with love and compassion. They will always empower you and foster independence. So if you sense or feel anything critical, judgmental, angry or negative, be certain it is not your angel. Just close down.

Even if you are channelling an angel other than your

own Guardian, they will usually come in quietly and gently. However, when the angel you have connected with has a vibration very different from that with which you are familiar, it may feel strange. You may feel shaky or as if you have expanded. Trust your intuition. Close down if you are afraid or in doubt.

When you have done a channelling with your angel you will carry more light in your energy fields. Light contains spiritual information, knowledge and love. Channelling will always help to expand you.

While your angel is close you may sense his presence, or picture a colour or smell a perfume. You may hear words but you are more likely to have a telepathic communication. Impressions may be given to you or pictures may come into your mind. Higher beings communicate in many ways. Stay open and receptive.

Angels are not fortune-tellers. High spiritual beings often decline to tell you your future. In any case, like any psychic, they could only tell you of a possible future, for your future is shaped by your thoughts, words and actions. The pathway ahead of you could go in any number of directions. A good psychic can only tell you what will probably happen based on the energy you are sending out at the time of consultation. You have the power to change it.

Of course, there are certain pre-life decisions which your soul took before you were born. You may have decided to experience bereavement at a certain age or to meet and marry a particular person. Even these soul decisions are not always set in stone.

It is permissible to ask your angel for guidance about your next step. You could tune in to Archangel Gabriel and request information about your life mission, if it is in your highest interest to know. You can ask what you are learning in a certain situation or for insights about relationships, problems and world situations. You can always ask for guidance about how you can best serve the planet.

One way of channelling your angel is to write a letter to him about your situation and what you want to know. Then make yourself receptive and write down whatever comes to you.

Another way is to do it with a partner, so that you can hold the energy for each other. In this case you will tell your partner what questions you want to ask. Your angel and your partner's angel will work together and your partner will channel any response.

To channel the angels

1. The questioner decides on his questions.
2. Ground yourself by feeling the floor through your feet.
3. Spend a few moments appreciating everything good in your life.
4. Visualise yourself in a beautiful place.
5. Surround yourself in white violet light to protect and raise your frequency.
6. Imagine a shaft of light flowing into your right brain and bathing the cells. Let it flow into your left brain, connecting both hemispheres of your brain.
7. Connect to your angel.
8. The questioner asks the questions.
9. Channel whatever is given to you by the angel.

Angel Balls

The angels can work with your energy to make miracles happen. I love to make angel humming balls, which are very simple and very powerful, and it is a lovely exercise to do with a group. You make a ball of sound and colour which you invite the angels to fill with their light.

If you know someone who feels lonely or has had a heartbreak, focus on the colour pink and direct the angels of love to fill your ball with their compassion and love.

Cynthia told me that her sister, Jean, was very upset after her husband left her. She cried all the time and could not get over it. At a workshop Cynthia made an angel love ball for her sister and sent it to her. When she called on her sister on the way home, Jean smiled at her for the first time since her husband left and from that moment started to live again.

At one workshop we made angel peace balls. I asked everyone to think of the colour they associated with peace and to invite the angels of colour to help them. They hummed into the ball and invited the angels of sound to work with them. Then we invoked the Angels of Peace to add their light.

A year later I returned to the same place and one of the participants told me that he had sent his golden peace ball to his mother, who had been in deep depression since his brother died. At the time he sent it she was sitting at home in her sitting room. To her amazement she saw a golden light hovering round the room. Her depression lifted completely and she was able to resume her life.

On another occasion, a young man wrote me a similar story. His mother was still grieving for his brother. He made a pink healing ball at a workshop for his mother. When he sent it she 'saw' it and felt comforted by it.

Sometimes we make beautiful vibrantly coloured balls of joy and throw them to people and places which need to be cheered. The Angels of Joy always love to participate in this.

Healing balls also contain the possibility of miracles. The love and focus you put into the ball as you add colour and sound enables the angelic forces to connect to the other person through you. A friend sent a deep blue healing ball to her uncle who was hobbling about after a knee injury and it got better more quickly than anyone had expected.

You can make a power ball and send it to someone who is nervous about an interview. I have done this and it really did give the man I sent it to courage. Or send a power ball to someone who is taking exams and it will hold them steady.

You can energise an abundance ball or one for love, prosperity, success, family harmony or even happiness and confidence.

If you are making a power ball or a peace ball and handing it to someone you know, place it in their solar plexus. If it is a love ball, place it in their heart. If you are asking the angels to help someone with their trust levels or their ability to communicate, place the humming ball in their throat centre. If someone feels unsafe and you are making an angel safety ball for them, place it in their base centre. If in doubt about where in the recipient to place your ball, ask the angels for guidance and act intuitively.

It is possible for several people to make an angel humming ball and then join them together into one huge one. This has a real impact when it is sent out.

Occasionally, at a workshop, all the participants create a humming ball and we send them to a trouble spot. It is a joyous feeling to sense or see the different coloured balls of light, all radiating their own vibration, bouncing into the challenged area and helping to bring peace, healing, empowerment, joy, confidence, calmness and a million other qualities into that place.

One reason that humming balls are so effective is that you are holding the focus and intention for some time. When you call in Angels of Sound they will take the perfect note from your singing, humming or toning and use it. In the same way, the Angels of Colour will take the perfect shade from the colour you are sending. And of course the Angels of the quality you are focusing on are also helping.

Sending a humming ball

1. Decide who you are sending the angel ball to and what quality your ball is to contain. Decide on the colour you are sending.
2. Close your eyes and rub your hands together, to open the hand chakras and build up energy.
3. Move your hands about a foot apart until you can feel

a sensation of resistance or cold or warmth or a
tingling feeling.

4. Think or visualise the colour you are using and invoke
   the angels of colour to work with you.
5. Invoke the Angels of whichever quality you are
   sending to add their light.
6. Hum into the ball and call in the Angels of Sound to
   work with you. Do this for as long as seems appropriate.
7. Send the ball to a person or place and picture it being
   absorbed.
8. Thank the angels.

Develop your Base Chakra with Archangel Gabriel

Archangel Gabriel and his twin flame, Hope, are in charge of the development of the base and sacral chakras. They aim to help everyone to move from a life based on survival and reaction, through joy and trust, to a life in blissful service.

At a physical level the base chakra governs the large intestine, rectum, legs and feet. Lower back pain indicates that you feel unsupported and are insecure about your life.

When it is working properly, the red third-dimensional base chakra gives you thrust and energy to get things done, to energise your work and relationships and have the passion to make a success of your life.

This chakra governs the working of the adrenal gland. As the chakra develops, the gland relaxes and only sends out extra adrenaline when you really need it. Your stress levels automatically drop and life flows smoothly and peacefully.

As you bring more joy into your life, Archangel Gabriel helps you to bring in the luminous pearl-white fourth-dimensional chakra. This lights up the cells of your body.

As the platinum fifth-dimensional chakra develops, Archangel Gabriel enables you to base your life on a strong spiritual foundation.

Your thoughts and the way you live your life are, naturally, most important in the development of the higher chakras. However, you can use movement, visualisation, sound, affirmation and invocation to accelerate the bringing-in of the higher chakras. Archangel Gabriel will help you to do this.

Exercise to anchor and activate the higher base chakras

Archangel Gabriel has most influence on a Friday, so this is the most powerful day to do this exercise.

1. Make sure you are in a place where you will be undisturbed.
2. If possible, raise the energy with flowers, a candle, sacred music if you like it and beautiful objects or books.
3. Before you start, stretch, loosen your neck with some gentle head rolls and shake out your body.
4. Kneel on both knees. If you cannot do this, sit on a chair.
5. Invoke the mighty Archangel Gabriel and his twin flame, Hope, to help you to develop your base chakra.
6. Rub your back at the base of your spine, where your base chakra is situated, until you can feel it tingle.
7. **To bring in the fourth-dimensional chakra:**
   a) Picture the red chakra of survival moving down your legs into your feet.
   b) Then visualise a luminous ball of pearl-white light above your head.
   c) Bring it down into your base chakra.

8. To bring in the fifth-dimensional chakra:
   a) Picture the red chakra moving down from your feet into the Earth. Then take the pearl-white chakra from your base to your feet and visualise a magnificent ball of platinum light, filled with bliss, above your head. Bring this down into your base chakra.
   b) Breathe several times into the base chakra, in-out-hold, in-out-hold.
   c) Open the petals of the flower on the in-breath and close them on the out-breath.

9. To activate the chakra physically, on the out-breath, squeeze the base of your spine with your buttocks and move it forward. Bow your head down.

10. On the in-breath, relax the base of your spine and bring it back and bring your head up and back. Do this four times. Relax.

11. For the fourth-dimensional chakra affirm I AM joy.

12. For the fifth-dimensional chakra affirm I AM bliss. Note that bliss means blessed, so you might prefer to affirm I AM blessed.

13. Tone the sound 'uh' into the base chakra.

14. Ask Archangel Gabriel and Hope to soothe, relax and heal your adrenals.

15. Visualise Archangel Gabriel and Hope putting a ball of light into this chakra.

16. Sit quietly as you focus on this chakra.

17. Thank Archangel Gabriel and Hope for the help you have received.

18. Put a golden egg of protection around yourself *or* continue to work on the other chakras.

Develop your Sacral Chakra with Archangel Gabriel

Archangel Gabriel and his twin flame, Hope, are in charge of the development of the base and sacral chakras. Originally humans, like animals, had only a base chakra, but as their consciousness grew, the sacral chakra of emotions and sexuality developed.

At a physical level the sacral chakra governs the bladder, bowels and sexual organs. We hold our beliefs about sexuality, food and emotions here. It controls the sexual glands, the gonads, ovaries and testes. When this chakra is working properly, menstruation and menopause flow easily, as do all hormonal changes for men as well as women.

When it is working properly, the orange third-dimensional sacral chakra enables you to have warm, comfortable friendships and good sexual relationships. You will feel good about yourself emotionally and be balanced about food.

As you balance your masculine and feminine energy, the fourth-dimensional sacral chakra starts to develop. If you invoke Archangel Gabriel, he will help you to find this balance.

When you develop your Goddess energy, the divine feminine in both male and female, the fifth-dimensional chakra, which is magenta, with platinum, starts to descend.

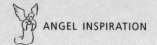

This exercise uses movement, visualisation, sound, affirmation and invocation to accelerate the bringing-in of the higher sacral chakras.

Exercise to anchor and activate the higher sacral chakras

Archangel Gabriel has most influence on a Friday, so this is the most powerful day to do this exercise.

1. Make sure you are in a place where you will be undisturbed.
2. If possible, raise the energy with flowers, a candle, appropriate angelic music if you like it and beautiful objects or books.
3. Before you start, stretch and shake out your body.
4. Kneel or sit cross-legged. If you cannot do this, sit on a chair.
5. Invoke the mighty Archangel Gabriel and his twin flame, Hope, to help you to develop your sacral chakra.
6. Rub your abdomen at the front and back, until you can feel it tingle.

To bring in the fourth-dimensional chakra:
   a) Picture the orange chakra moving down your legs into your ankles.
   b) Visualise a luminous ball of pale pink-orange light above your head.
   c) Bring it down into your sacral chakra.

To bring in the fifth-dimensional chakra:
   a) Picture the orange chakra moving down from your ankles into the Earth.
   b) Take the pink-orange chakra from your abdomen into your ankles.

c) Visualise a magnificent ball of magenta and plat-
        inum light, the divine feminine, above your head.
    d) Bring this down into your sacral chakra.

7. Breathe several times into the sacral chakra, in-out-
    hold, in-out-hold. Open the petals of the flower on
    the in-breath and close them on the out-breath.

8. To activate the chakra physically, move into the cat
    position. On the out-breath, bring down your head
    and hump up your back. Squeeze your abdomen.

9. On the in-breath, bring up your head and bottom.
    Open the chakra. Do this four times. Relax.

10. For the fourth-dimensional chakra affirm I AM
    balance.

11. For the fifth-dimensional chakra affirm I AM the
    divine feminine.

12. Tone the sound 'ooh' into the sacral chakra.

13. Ask Archangel Gabriel and his twin flame, Hope, to
    soothe, relax and heal your sexual glands. Even if you
    no longer have them, they are still working in the
    etheric.

14. Visualise Archangel Gabriel and Hope putting a ball of
    light into this chakra.

15. Sit quietly as you focus on this chakra.

16. Thank Archangel Gabriel and Hope for the help you
    have received.

17. Put a golden egg of protection around yourself *or*
    continue to work on the other chakras.

Develop Your Solar Plexus Chakra with Archangel Uriel

Archangel Uriel and his twin flame, Aurora, are in charge of the development of the solar plexus, which is the centre of personal power and wisdom.

At a physical level this chakra governs the liver, spleen, stomach, gall bladder and pancreas. We hold our fears and lack of confidence in this chakra. When it is working properly, at a third-dimensional level, you feel confident and empowered.

This chakra governs the pancreas and when this chakra is in balance you are able to give and receive nurturing on every level.

As you master your fears and connect with your wisdom, your fourth-dimensional chakra starts to develop. It is gold. If you invoke Archangel Uriel, he will help you to release your fears and to become wise.

The fifth-dimensional chakra is gold with rainbow lights. You now connect to Universal wisdom.

This exercise uses movement, visualisation, sound, affirmation and invocation to accelerate the bringing-in of the higher solar plexus chakras.

Exercise to anchor and activate the higher solar plexus chakras

Archangel Uriel has most influence on a Thursday, which is the most powerful day to do this exercise.

1. Make sure you are in a place where you will be undisturbed.
2. If possible, raise the energy with flowers, a candle, angelic music if you like it and beautiful objects or books.
3. Before you start, stretch and shake out your body.
4. Kneel or sit cross-legged. If you cannot do this, sit on a chair.
5. Invoke the mighty Archangel Uriel and his twin flame, Aurora, to help you to develop your solar plexus chakra.
6. Rub your solar plexus in front and behind your back, until you can feel it tingle.

To bring in the fourth-dimensional chakra:
   a) Picture the yellow chakra moving down your legs into your calves.
   b) Visualise a pure gold ball of light above your head.
   c) Bring it down into your solar plexus.

To bring in the fifth-dimensional chakra
   a) Picture the yellow chakra moving down your calves into the Earth.
   b) Take the gold chakra from your solar plexus down to your calves.
   c) Visualise a wondrous ball of gold with rainbow lights above your head.
   d) Bring this down into your solar plexus.

7. Breathe several times into the solar plexus, in and out evenly. Open the petals of the flower on the in-breath and close them on the out-breath.

8. To activate the chakra physically, bring your hands up to your shoulders and lift your elbows. Breathe out, hold the breath, twist left, come back to centre, breathe in, hold the breath, twist right. Come back to centre. Do this four times. Relax.

9. Repeat the exercise starting by twisting to the right. Relax.

10. For the fourth-dimensional chakra affirm I AM wise.

11. For the fifth-dimensional chakra affirm I AM a Master of wisdom.

12. Tone the sound 'oh' into the heart.

13. Ask Archangel Uriel and his twin flame, Aurora, to soothe, relax, strengthen and heal your pancreas.

14. Visualise Archangel Uriel putting a ball of light into this chakra.

15. Sit quietly as you focus on this chakra.

16. Thank Archangel Uriel and Aurora for the help you have received.

17. Put a golden egg of protection around yourself *or* continue to work on the other chakras.

Develop your Heart Chakra with Archangel Chamuel

Archangel Chamuel and his twin flame, Charity, are in charge of the development of the heart chakra. This is the centre of love.

At a physical level this chakra governs the heart, chest, lungs, shoulders, arms and hands. If we feel unloved, unlovable or rejected, we close down our heart chakra and cause problems in these areas of our body. When it is working properly, the green heart chakra, which has a pure pink centre, opens and you radiate warmth and love. You automatically become a healer.

This chakra governs the thymus gland. When your heart centre is open your immune system is strong.

As you open your heart to unconditional love and acceptance of others, your fourth-dimensional chakra starts to develop. If you invoke Archangel Chamuel, he will help you to forgive and release the past and expand the flame of love in your heart.

The fifth-dimensional chakra is white. You now carry Christ Consciousness.

This exercise uses movement, visualisation, sound, affirmation and invocation to accelerate the bringing-in of the higher heart chakras.

Exercise to anchor and activate the higher heart chakras
Archangel Chamuel has most influence on a Monday, which is the most powerful day to do this exercise.

1. Make sure you are in a place where you will be undisturbed.
2. If possible, raise the energy with flowers, a candle, angelic music if you like it and beautiful objects or books.
3. Before you start, stretch and shake out your body.
4. Kneel or sit cross-legged. If you cannot do this, sit on a chair.
5. Invoke the mighty Archangel Chamuel and his twin flame, Charity, to help you to develop your heart chakra.
6. Rub your chest at the front and your back behind it, until you can feel it tingle.

To bring in the fourth-dimensional chakra:
   a) Picture the green chakra moving down your legs into your knees.
   b) Visualise a luminous pale violet-pink ball of light above your head.
   c) Bring it down into your heart chakra.

To bring in the fifth-dimensional chakra:
   a) Picture the green chakra moving down from your knees into the Earth.
   b) Take the violet-pink chakra from your heart down to your knees.
   c) Visualise a magnificent ball of pure shimmering white, above your head.
   d) Bring this down into your heart.

7. Breathe several times into the heart, in and out evenly.

Open the petals of the flower on the in-breath and close them on the out-breath.

8. To activate the chakra physically, bring your hands in front of your heart and clasp them together, with your elbows out to the side. On the out-breath bring your left elbow down and feel a squeeze at the back of your heart chakra. On the in-breath bring your right elbow down. Do this three times, ending with an out-breath. Hold it and bring your elbows parallel. Pull them apart and feel the squeeze at the back of your heart chakra. Release your breath.

   Repeat this, starting by bringing your right elbow down first.

9. For the fourth-dimensional chakra affirm I AM love.

10. For the fifth-dimensional chakra affirm I AM unconditional love.

11. Tone the sound 'ah' into the heart.

12. Ask Archangel Chamuel and Charity to soothe, relax, strengthen and heal your thymus.

13. Visualise Archangel Chamuel putting a ball of light into this chakra.

14. Sit quietly as you focus on this chakra.

15. Thank Archangel Chamuel and Charity for the help you have received.

16. Put a golden egg of protection around yourself *or* continue to work on the other chakras.

Develop Your Throat Chakra with Archangel Michael

Archangel Michael and his twin flame, Faith, are in charge of the development of the throat chakra. This is the centre of trust, communication, will and integrity.

At a physical level this chakra governs the throat and neck. When you resist life's experiences or feel unable to communicate honestly, you develop sore throats or find the back of your neck is stiff. When it is working properly, the turquoise third-dimensional chakra opens and you communicate easily and with integrity. You start to tune in to higher guidance from your Higher Self.

The throat chakra governs the thyroid gland. When your throat centre is working properly your metabolism is perfect for your body.

As you open your throat centre in alignment with your higher will, your fourth-dimensional chakra starts to develop. This is deep blue violet. If you invoke Archangel Michael, he will help you find the courage, strength, trust and faith to speak your truth.

The fifth-dimensional chakra is deep blue violet. You now develop higher psychic and spiritual gifts.

This exercise uses movement, visualisation, sound, affirmation and invocation to accelerate the bringing-in of the higher throat chakras.

Exercise to anchor and activate the higher throat chakras

Archangel Michael has most influence on a Tuesday, which is the most powerful day to do this exercise.

1. Make sure you are in a place where you will be undisturbed.
2. If possible, raise the energy with flowers, a candle, angelic music if you like it and beautiful objects or books.
3. Before you start, stretch and shake out your body.
4. Kneel or sit cross-legged. If you cannot do this, sit on a chair.
5. Invoke the mighty Archangel Michael and his twin flame, Faith, to help you to develop your throat chakra.
6. Rub your throat and the back of your neck, until you can feel it tingle.

To bring in the fourth-dimensional chakra:
   a) Picture the turquoise chakra moving down your legs above your knees.
   b) Visualise a deep blue-violet ball of light above your head.
   c) Bring it down into your throat chakra.

To bring in the fifth-dimensional chakra:
   a) Picture the turquoise chakra moving from above your knees into the Earth.
   b) Take the deep blue-violet chakra from your throat down to above your knees.
   c) Visualise a magnificent ball of royal blue light above your head.
   d) Bring this down into your throat.

i) Breathe several times into the throat. The breathing is out-in-hold. Open the petals of the flower on the in-breath and close them on the out-breath.

ii) To activate the chakra physically, bring your chin down into your thyroid on the out-breath and squeeze. Then bring up your head on the in-breath. Repeat this. The fourth time, hold your chin down and count to sixteen. Bring up your head. Relax

iii) For the fourth-dimensional chakra affirm I CLAIM MY PSYCHIC AND SPIRITUAL GIFTS.

iv) For the fifth-dimensional chakra affirm I AM A CO-CREATOR WITH THE DIVINE.

7. Tone the sound 'ee' into the throat.

8. Ask Archangel Michael and Faith to soothe, relax, strengthen and heal your thyroid.

9. Visualise Archangel Michael putting a ball of light into this chakra.

10. Sit quietly as you focus on this chakra.

11. Thank Archangel Michael and Faith for the help you have received.

12. Put a golden egg of protection around yourself *or* continue to work on the other chakras.

Develop Your Third-eye Chakra with Archangel Raphael

Archangel Raphael and his twin flame, Mary, are in charge of the development of the third-eye chakra of intuition and divine connection.

At a physical level this chakra governs the eyes, ears, sinuses, head and nose. Headaches or problems in this area indicate a blockage in this chakra. When this indigo chakra is working freely, you become intuitive or clairvoyant. You are able to heal with your thoughts and words.

This chakra governs the pituitary gland, which is the master gland for the whole body. When this chakra is working in alignment, you look and feel youthful and are mentally alert, open-minded and healthy. If you invoke Archangel Raphael, he will help you to develop your inner vision.

The fourth-dimensional chakra is golden-white and your thoughts and visions now align with the Divine. The fifth-dimensional chakra is crystal clear.

This exercise uses movement, visualisation, sound, affirmation and invocation to accelerate the bringing-in of the higher throat chakras.

Exercise to anchor and activate the higher third-eye chakras

Archangel Raphael has most influence on a Wednesday, which is the most powerful day to do this exercise.

1. Make sure you are in a place where you will be undisturbed.
2. If possible, raise the energy with flowers, a candle, appropriate angelic music if you like it and beautiful objects or books.
3. Mentally say thank you for your blessings.
4. Before you start, stretch and shake out your body.
5. Kneel or sit cross-legged. If you cannot do this, sit on a chair.
6. Invoke the mighty Archangel Raphael and his twin flame, Mary, to help you to develop your third-eye chakra.
7. Energise your hands by rubbing them together. Then gently massage your face, especially your hairline, sinuses and eyes, temples, jaw and ears. Rub your forehead and the back of your head, until you can feel it tingle.

To bring in the fourth-dimensional chakra:
   a) Picture the indigo chakra moving down to your legs.
   b) Visualise a golden-white ball of light above your head.
   c) Bring it down into your third eye.

To bring in the fifth-dimensional chakra:
   a) Picture the indigo chakra moving from your legs into the Earth.
   b) Take the golden-white chakra from your third eye down to above your legs.

c) Visualise a magnificent ball of crystal-clear light above your head.

    d) Bring this down into your third eye.

8. Breathe several times into the third eye. The breathing is out-in-hold. Open the petals of the flower on the in-breath and close them on the out-breath.

9. To activate the chakra physically, bring your hands together in front of your throat centre. Squeeze a breath from base centre up your body as if squeezing a tube of toothpaste. Bring your hands up with the breath and hold it opposite your third eye. Release it through your crown. Repeat this if you wish to. Relax.

10. For the fourth-dimensional chakra affirm GOD AND I ARE ONE.

11. For the fifth-dimensional chakra affirm I AM THAT I AM.

12. Tone the sound 'aye' into the third eye.

13. Ask Archangel Raphael and Mary to soothe, relax, strengthen and heal your pituitary gland.

14. Visualise Archangel Raphael putting a ball of light into this chakra.

15. Sit quietly as you focus on this chakra.

16. Thank Archangel Raphael and Mary for the help you have received.

17. Put a golden egg of protection around yourself *or* continue to work on the other chakras.

EXERCISE SEVENTEEN

Develop Your Crown Chakra with Archangel Jophiel

Archangel Jophiel and his twin flame, Christine, are in charge of the development of the crown chakra of connection to the Higher Self or soul.

At a physical level, when this chakra, the thousand-petalled lotus, is out of alignment, you feel off centre. When this violet chakra is working freely, you become attuned to your higher purpose.

This chakra governs the pineal gland, which takes in and stores light. Light contains spiritual information and knowledge. When this chakra is open you feel totally connected to your soul. If you invoke Archangel Jophiel, he will illuminate your mind and fill you with wisdom.

The fourth-dimensional chakra is white-violet and you align with your monad or I AM Presence. The fifth-dimensional crown is merged with the third eye and is a blazing diamond of light.

This exercise uses movement, visualisation, sound, affirmation and invocation to accelerate the bringing-in of the higher crown chakras.

Exercise to anchor and activate the higher crown chakras

Archangel Jophiel has most influence on a Sunday, which is the most powerful day to do this exercise.

1. Make sure you are in a place where you will be undisturbed.
2. If possible, raise the energy with flowers, a candle, angelic music if you like it and beautiful objects or books.
3. Before you start, stretch and shake out your body.
4. Kneel or sit cross-legged. If you cannot do this, sit on a chair.
5. Invoke the mighty Archangel Jophiel and his twin flame, Christine, to help you to develop your crown chakra.
6. Gently rub the crown of your head and the base of your spine.

To bring in the fourth-dimensional chakra:

    a) Picture the violet chakra moving down to the top of your legs.

    b) Visualise a white-violet ball of light above your head.

    c) Bring it down into your crown.

To bring in the fifth-dimensional chakra:

    a) Picture the violet chakra moving from your legs into the Earth.

    b) Take the white-violet chakra from your crown down to the top of your legs.

    c) Visualise a magnificent diamond above your head.

    d) Bring this down into your crown.

7. There is no breathing or exercise for this chakra. Simply bend your head and surrender to the Divine.
8. Sound the ohm and visualise it moving upwards to Source.

Develop Your Seat of the Soul Chakra with Archangel Zadkiel

The eighth chakra is the seat of the soul. It is about a foot above your head, is blue-white in colour and relates to your auric space. Through this chakra you connect to your Higher Self or soul for guidance.

The seat of the soul chakra contains soul information, which it then downloads into your chakra system.

As you bring down your fourth-dimensional chakras, it descends into the crown and temporarily doubles up with the crown chakra.

Exercise

1. Sit and breathe quietly until you are calm and centred.
2. Physically reach up and sense yourself holding the blue-white ball of light above your head. Then drop your arms and relax them.
3. Invoke Archangel Zadkiel and his twin flame, Amethyst, to help you bring down your soul energy.
4. Visualise the light radiating down from the seat of the soul chakra, through each of your chakras in turn. Pause as the light comes into each chakra. It is downloading information from your soul.
5. Imagine the chakras turning into a column of light.
6. Thank Archangel Zadkiel and Amethyst for helping you.

Meditation for Dispensation from the Lords of Karma

1. Make sure you are in a place where you will be undisturbed.
2. If possible, raise the energy with flowers, a candle, appropriate music if you like it and beautiful objects or books.
3. Sit or lie with your back straight.
4. Ground yourself by imagining roots reaching down from your feet into the Earth.
5. Relax and let go of the outside world. Ask your Guardian Angel to enfold and support you. Imagine your angel stroking your head and relaxing away all the tension. Then feel your neck, shoulders arms and hands being gently stroked. Take this feeling down slowly through your body until you feel comfortable and secure.
6. A magnificent white marble staircase is now appearing in front of you and you find yourself walking up it easily and effortlessly. You are going higher and higher until you find yourself at level thirty-three. This is the sacred level of Christ consciousness. Rest here in unconditional love.

   A host of angels is coming to collect you. They are lovingly leading you forward and upward until you

reach the steps of a magnificent temple. This is the temple of the Lords of Karma. The angels are waiting here for you. Go up the steps alone and across the courtyard, which is surrounded by colourful flowers. There is a beautiful fountain in the centre. Pause here.

A monk with a radiantly peaceful face is approaching. He silently greets you and leads you to a door. Knock on the door and enter. The Lords of Karma await you. The seven mighty Lords of Karma are seated round a table.

Approach and reverently ask if part or all of your personal or family karma can be transmuted.

7. Be open to any impressions or response from the powerful Lords of Karma. Remember that they are merciful.
8. Be open to any message they wish to offer you.
9. Thank them.
10. Leave the chamber and allow the monk to conduct you back across the courtyard and down the steps to where your angels wait to lead you back to your physical life on Earth.
11. Sit quietly and reflect on what you have experienced. Note any sensations in your physical body.
12. Wriggle your fingers and toes. Stretch and open your eyes.

Releasing Your Vows

Vows are often made with ritual or ceremony, in front of witnesses. This is what sets them so strongly in your consciousness and calls in the angels to help you keep your vow, through lifetimes if necessary. An angel is assigned to oversee every vow you make.

If you are still being influenced by past marriage vows, contracts, oaths, curses or any other vow in this life, it is helpful to release them. A marriage is a ceremony. A divorce often does not release the energy of the original contract.

In past lives you may have made vows which are still locked into you and affect your life. Here are some possibilities: vows of poverty, obedience, chastity, silence, charity, fidelity, austerity, conformity or penitence. You may have given or received a curse or damnation.

Visualisation to release vows

1. Make sure you are in a place where you will be undisturbed.
2. If possible, raise the energy with flowers, a candle, appropriate music if you like it and beautiful objects or books.
3. Sit or lie with your back straight.

4. Ground yourself by imagining roots reaching down from your feet into the Earth.

5. Relax and let go of the outside world. Ask your Guardian Angel to support you.

6. Breathe away the tension in your body and surround yourself with a pink light.

7. Visualise or think yourself back in the place where you made your original vow *or* take yourself into a magnificent temple. Look around and get the feel of the place.

8. Be aware of anyone taking the vow with you and of the person conducting the ceremony.

9. Look at the congregation, which is supporting your vow. If you have had many past lives where you took vows, there may be hundreds or even thousands of people from other lives still holding your vow in place with their energy.

10. Hand any ring or symbol of a vow back to the person who gave it to you.

11. If you had a chastity belt, or even several, placed on you, it is still active in the etheric, as are cloaks, uniforms, hair shirts, begging bowls or any other symbol you assumed at that time.

12. Clearly and positively tell the person who conducted the original ceremony or ceremonies, anyone who you were bound to and the congregation, that you are now releasing yourself from the vow and all its commitment. Allow them to clap and applaud your decision.

13. Light a candle either in your imagination or reality to symbolise your freedom.

14. Thank the angels who have continued to support your vow and release them.

15. Walk out of the place where you are into the sunshine. Have a party or do something you really enjoy to celebrate your new life.

16. Open your eyes and smile. You are free!

Visiting the Archangel Chambers

Each of the Archangels has a special place in the etheric of the planet, which you can visit in meditation or sleep. If you ask to go to one of their temples, they will work on you.

When you go to sleep at night your spirit leaves your body and travels to a variety of places. We know this unconsciously for we say of someone who is deeply asleep, 'He's gone' or 'He's far away.'

It is helpful to direct your spirit to visit places which will enhance your spiritual growth. Do this before you go to sleep. You simply say, for example, 'I direct my spirit to visit Archangel Michael's temple tonight to give me courage and strength for my new project,' or 'Please take me to Archangel Uriel's chamber in Poland tonight for the release of my fear of heights.' They will give you all that is possible under spiritual law.

The Archangel Chambers are in the etheric above the following places. If you have physically been to any one of these places, the Archangel of that place has drawn you into his influence.

Archangel Michael	Banff, Canada
Archangel Jophiel	South of the Great Wall of China
Archangel Chamuel	St Louis, Missouri
Archangel Gabriel	Mount Shasta, California

Archangel Raphael	Fatima, Portugal
Archangel Uriel	Tatra Mountains, Poland
Archangel Zadkiel	Cuba

You can leave your request general or ask for specific help.

Archangel Michael	For courage, strength and psychic or physical protection
Archangel Jophiel	For wisdom, illumination, help with learning or teaching
Archangel Chamuel	For help with forgiveness, to gain more compassion or empathy. To open your heart.
Archangel Gabriel	For purification, guidance, to put more order into your life
Archangel Raphael	For healing, abundance, help with travel and to develop inner vision
Archangel Uriel	For inner peace and release of fears
Archangel Zadkiel	For transmutation, joy and mercy

Meditation to Visit an Archangel Chamber

1. Make sure you are in a place where you will be undisturbed.
2. If possible, raise the energy with flowers, a candle, angelic music if you like it and beautiful objects or books.
3. Sit or lie with your back straight.
4. Ground yourself by imagining roots reaching down from your feet into the Earth.

5. Relax and let go of the outside world.
6. Tell the angels to take you to the Archangel Chamber of your choice and the purpose of your visit.
7. Visualise, sense or feel the angels surrounding you and taking you up, up through the ethers, through the stars.
8. Ahead is a magnificent shimmering temple, surrounded by light.
9. Walk up the steps of the temple and a beautiful angel meets you at the top. She washes your feet and gives you a pure white robe to wear.
10. Then follow her along gracious corridors to a vast hall.
11. The Archangel is sitting on a throne, radiating glory.
12. You may approach and experience his presence.
13. State your purpose and await a response.
14. Thank him and leave the great hall.
15. The angels take you back through the corridors and fly with you through the ethers back into your body.
16. Stretch and make sure you are grounded. Open your eyes.

Anchoring the Higher Rays

As the consciousness of humanity rapidly expands, higher rays are becoming available to us. In a meditation one morning dolphins started leaping at me. It was exhilarating and exciting. Beautiful silvery angels appeared with them. I was told to bring in the platinum ray and anchor it through my body. I did so.

I learnt that when Atlantis sank, the dolphins became keepers of the platinum ray until such time as humanity was ready to receive it again. The time is now.

It is an ascension ray, filling you with the vibrations of bliss and enabling you to live a spiritual life out in the world. When you anchor the platinum ray and carry it in your body, your aura touches others and enables them to receive it also. You identify yourself as a team leader, helping many to ascension.

Meditation to Anchor the Platinum Ray

1. Make sure you are in a place where you will be undisturbed.
2. If possible, raise the energy with flowers, a candle, angelic music if you like it and beautiful objects or books.
3. Sit or lie with your back straight.

4. Ground yourself by imagining roots reaching down from your feet into the Earth.
5. Relax and let go of the outside world.
6. Visualise yourself swimming safely in a beautiful clear blue ocean. It can be as shallow or deep as you like and you are totally safe.
7. Dolphins approach you. They play with you and communicate with you. Enjoy their company.
8. They are sending energy to your base chakra and preparing it to anchor the platinum ray.
9. Return to the shore and stand on the golden sand under a blue sky. The sun is warm and healing. Open your arms to receive.
10. The platinum ray is coming down through your crown and into your base chakra. Then it continues to flow through you to the earth. Relax deeply into bliss and joy.
11. Dedicate yourself to being a worthy carrier of this ray.
12. Thank the angels and dolphins.
13. Open your eyes and stretch.

You may also call in the eighth ray, which is aquamarine. This is the ray for planetary cleansing.

It is important for as many people as possible to anchor the twelfth ray, which is the gold ray of Christ. It is deep gold, very protective, and carries Christ consciousness.

The diamond ray is now available to those dedicated to the ascension pathway. It is the ray of total purity, oneness and all knowing wisdom. It carries unconditional love. You may ask for this to be anchored in your crown and it will speed your spiritual journey.